PREACHING
HOLINESS

PREACHING
HOLINESS

Pastoral
Considerations

JEREN ROWELL

THE FOUNDRY
PUBLISHING

Cover design: Rob Monacelli
Interior design: Sharon Page

Library of Congress Cataloging-in-Publication Data
A complete catalog record for this book is available from the Library of Congress.

Almighty God, to whom all hearts are open, all desires known,
and from whom no secrets are hidden:
Cleanse the thoughts of our hearts by the inspiration of your Holy Spirit,
that we may perfectly love you and worthily magnify your holy name.
Through Jesus Christ, our Lord. Amen.
—Collect for Purity, Book of Common Prayer

No condemnation now I dread,
Jesus, and all in him, is mine!
Alive in him, my living Head,
And clothed in righteousness divine,
Bold I approach the eternal throne,
And claim the crown, through Christ my own!
—Charles Wesley, "And Can It Be?"

■ CONTENTS

■ ACKNOWLEDGMENTS

This project arose from a pastor's resource day that I was privileged to facilitate for the Nebraska District of the Church of the Nazarene in August 2017. Therefore, thank you to District Superintendent Dan Cole and the pastors of the Nebraska District for the invitation and for your engaged participation in helping these thoughts be gathered in this way.

Not long before spending the day with the Nebraska pastors, I was sitting in a General Assembly plenary session, sketching an outline for the presentation. Sitting next to me was Bonnie Perry, editorial director for The Foundry Publishing. The conversation about what I was doing quickly turned to Bonnie's declarative invitation: "That's a book!" So thank you again to my good friend Bonnie, for your belief that I have something to say to the church.

Thanks also to my colleague at Nazarene Theological Seminary, Rev. Levi Jones, who read the manuscript and offered helpful suggestions.

And I am grateful to the congregations and mentors who shaped my preaching over many years and were a large part of not only teaching me how to preach holiness but also helping to form me in the pursuit of Christlikeness.

■ THE **WHO**, **WHAT**, AND **HOW** OF PREACHING

Pastors who identify in the Wesleyan-Holiness tradition may recognize some variation of this exchange:

> Parishioner: *"We don't hear holiness preaching anymore."*
>
> Pastor: *"What do you mean? I preach holiness every week!"*

This can be a frustrating conversation for conscientious pastors who believe they are faithfully preaching holiness of heart and life as proclaimed in the Scriptures and through the witness of the church. I have noticed that pastors can become defensive about this critique in ways that usually do not help the conversation proceed. Perhaps it elicits memories of being grilled by the credentials board on holiness theology.

So what is really going on here? I am not sure this exchange is about doctrine or even about biblical preaching. I suggest this *insider disconnect* between parishioner and pastor is about language or, to use a broader term, culture. I use the phrase *insider disconnect* here because we need to acknowledge the shaping presence of an insider culture that is the Holiness Movement as it gave birth to several denominational expressions, including the Church of the Nazarene. I find this noteworthy because most pastors will testify that they do not experience this insider disconnect with seekers or new Christians who generally know nothing of the language and culture of a holiness church. Therefore, they do not begin with preconceived ideas or expectations about how they are learning to know the fullness of God's provision for us in holiness of heart and life.

When I have listened carefully to people who say, "Our pastors do not preach holiness anymore," what I have discovered is that, often, there are certain terms or certain phrases they are not hearing that they have come to associate with holiness preaching. For example, *second-blessing holiness* is a phrase that at one time was ubiquitous and well loved but now brings puzzled expressions to the faces of new generations of holiness people. The absence of that once-familiar language is viewed by some as a failure to teach, preach, or guide adequately our young people into a vibrant experience of heart holiness. There is certainly serious responsibility to be accepted all around in this regard.

However, in perhaps hundreds of discussions I have engaged with young people preparing for ministry, I have discovered that their puzzled looks do not come because they do not believe in a sanctifying act of God "subsequent to regeneration;"[1] rather, they are simply unfamiliar with the particular language and much of the culture from which that belief was born. Additionally, there are others who do know the cultural language but prefer to reach more directly into the language of Scripture in ways that speak less of a dramatic experience and more of being formed in the character of Christ. (Please do not assume that I will argue process against crisis here. Both are involved.)

There is no particular deficit that should be attached to this lack of familiarity with the culture of the American Holiness Movement. Additionally, those of us with much history in the movement must recognize that communicating holiness in changing contexts may require new language to proclaim faithfully the "old, old story." The point here is simply that the disconnect we sometimes lament between clergy and laity or between generations around the proclamation of holiness doctrine and experience is not typically a disconnect of belief or conviction but one of language and culture.

---

1. From Article of Faith X, "Christian Holiness and Entire Sanctification," *Manual of the Church of the Nazarene 2017–2021* (Kansas City: Nazarene Publishing House), 31.

This disconnect is precisely why the pastoral skill of preaching holiness with clarity and conviction is so important and so much in need of renewal for our time. Vital holiness preaching cannot rise from obligation, cannot occur simply because it is our distinguishing doctrine and *ought* to be preached. Holiness preaching that moves people, under the work of the Holy Spirit, to know and experience the fullness of God's provision for us in Christ Jesus must rise from the preacher's passionate and intimate personal knowledge of the love of God that saves and sanctifies, forming us more and more into the image of the Lord Jesus.

Could it be that holiness preaching has lost some of its voice in our time because we have too often approached holiness preaching as an *apologetic*[2] rather than from pastoral love? This happens when the idea of apologetic is reduced to some kind of "scientism" approach to proclamation, where winning the argument is the goal. When proclamation is delivered not only with logical precision but also with pastoral love, it can become the best kind of apologetic, one that woos and wins rather than seeking to manipulate or control. That is to say, if we approach holiness preaching only in terms of trying to convince people of the rightness of the doctrine, the preaching can quickly become dry, lifeless, and potentially combative. This kind of preaching is typically born of our own anxiety or unease with the subject.

However, if holiness preaching comes from the heart of a pastor who has gone to Scripture in service to a people she or he knows and loves, then the preaching has a chance to rise from the heart of a pastor who longs for people to know the freedom and joy of God's sanctifying grace. Of course, this premise assumes that the preacher personally knows and is living in the experience of holiness of heart and life. Perhaps that assumption should go without saying, but it cannot. The evidence, in terms of the fruit of the Spirit, has too often been lacking in the lives of our preachers and pastors—we who should be modeling it for our people. That lack creates what Dr. Mildred Wynkoop

---

2. Meaning a formal defense or justification.

called a "credibility gap,"[3] or a disconnect between what we proclaim and how it actually shows up in the attitudes and conduct of our lives. "The peculiarity of Wesleyan theology is its emphasis on holiness as personal experience."[4] This emphasis is why we must not reduce holiness preaching to merely explaining doctrine but must always allow it to proclaim the good news of freedom from sin and transformation of life. The doctrine of holiness "turns gangrenous apart from the constant flow of living blood out of the deepest heart."[5]

To think rightly about preaching holiness, we must not only think about *what* should be said (Scripture, doctrine) and *how* it should be said (culture, language, story, structure, and form), but we must also think deeply about *who* is doing the saying. In other words, Pastor, we cannot preach what we do not know. And when I say *know*, I have in mind the kind of knowing that the Bible describes in the deepest and most intimate ways. It is something deep and visceral, a knowing that goes beyond data alone and reaches to intuition, life wisdom, and experiential validation. I have always believed that faithful and effective preaching can only happen when the text of Scripture, through the present work of the Spirit, does its work first on the preacher. Only then, having encountered the living Word, can the preacher come with any authority to proclaim to the people of God: "Thus says the Lord." When this happens, the preaching is rich, beautiful, and life-giving. When it fails to happen, the preaching is tepid and impotent.

During my twelve years of serving as a district superintendent for the Church of the Nazarene, I sat hundreds of times with pastors and church boards to conduct a review of the health of a congregation and a church's ministry. I began by inviting board members to offer personal accountability for their leadership in terms of the statement of qualification given in the *Manual of the Church of the Nazarene*. First among

---

3. See chapter 3 of Wynkoop's *A Theology of Love: The Dynamic of Wesleyanism* (Kansas City: Beacon Hill Press of Kansas City, 1972), 39–52.

4. Ibid., 44.

5. Ibid.

the several questions is, "Are you living in the experience of entire sanctification?" The answer choices I gave were:

- I have no idea what this means.
- By the grace of God, yes, I am.
- I understand what it is, but I am really not living there.
- I want to know this, but I do not really understand sanctification.

Over the years I was amazed at how often the board members of our local churches were willing to answer honestly that they really had no meaningful understanding of what we mean by "entire sanctification." These revelations afforded me the opportunity to spend some time with them, talking not only about what the doctrine means but also sharing my own testimony with them and urging them to seek the Lord with all of their hearts, minds, souls, and strength so that they might know the joy of a life that is free from the tyranny of sin!

Without exception, I encountered people who responded to this good news with spiritual hunger and with what seemed a sense of relief that holiness is no dreadful obligation but a life-giving provision from God. Usually, the hesitation they articulated was rooted in the language of "entire," thinking it means "finished" or "nothing further needed." When they learned that the word entire in this context does not mean "it is all done" but something more like, "I am all in, by the grace of God," their faces lit up and their postures straightened as they realized the blessing that is God's sanctifying grace.

The purpose of this book is to help us connect the what and the how of holiness preaching with the who of the preacher's own knowledge and experience of the sanctified life. We have sufficient resources for the theological and exegetical work that must be done to be good holiness preachers. A faithful and effective holiness preacher will be immersed not only in the classic works of holiness theology but also in the more contemporary works of our recent and current theologians and teachers.

What I mean to do in this present work is to challenge and inspire us afresh to approach this task from a pastoral bearing that is something like what the apostle Paul expressed when he wrote to the Corinthian church, "We have . . . opened wide our hearts to you" (2 Cor. 6:11). There is no more compelling way to preach holiness than from a heart of authentic love, a deep desire that people under one's spiritual care would know and experience the life-transforming power of the perfect love of God in Christ. If we truly believe that the holiness message is a gospel word for our people, who so often are "harassed and helpless" (Matt. 9:36), then we will give ourselves as pastors to proclaiming this good news with clarity, conviction, and passion.

To this end, Pastor, I want to talk to you as a friend and mentor in these pages. This is certainly not about breaking any new theological or homiletical ground. It is a far humbler project. This is, perhaps, more about reminding us of a rich heritage that can continue to shape our missional engagement with the world, even while we necessarily learn the rhythms and language of post-Christian culture. This is about trying to inspire us as pastors to be unafraid to preach a message that is radically optimistic about what God wants to do for us.

My concern for us is that our people have been and are being shaped significantly by a Christian culture that too often sells short the transforming gospel of Jesus Christ. I have encountered thousands of Nazarenes, across years of traveling from church to church, who believe that the best they can do as followers of Jesus is to find themselves on a constant cycle of failure and forgiveness. It is a fairly pessimistic view of what it means to know and follow Jesus. The gift of God to us in the birth, life, death, resurrection, and ascension of our Lord Jesus is certainly more than "do the best you can until we get to heaven." The promise of the gospel is that "there is now no condemnation for those who are in Christ Jesus, because through Christ Jesus the law of the Spirit who gives life has set you free from the law of sin and death" (Rom. 8:1–2, emphasis mine).

Good news! And, that'll preach!

PART ONE

WHO Is Doing the Preaching?

1 THE TESTIMONY OF A HOLINESS PREACHER

All clergy in the Church of the Nazarene, and likely in most other groups as well, have stories to tell about the journey toward ordination, which typically involves an annual meeting with an area board of ministerial credentials. An essential part of this annual accountability, rightly so, is to hear the candidate's spiritual testimony. In holiness groups, this testimony must include a clear profession of the experience of entire sanctification.

When I was a candidate more than thirty-five years ago, we all knew that this testimony, in order to be judged sufficient, must include the ability to name the date and locate the place of our "crisis experience," our "second definite work of grace." This expectation was driven by the belief, which was supported by holiness preaching at the time, that the focal point of the sanctified life was an individual moment of consecration, usually at the altar (mourner's bench) of the church or camp meeting, when one "prayed through" to a crisis of full surrender of life to the lordship of Jesus Christ. This moment of consecration included the belief, experience, and testimony of the "infilling of the Holy Spirit," which cleansed the heart from sin and empowered one "for life and service." When one experienced this "second work of grace" (the "first work" usually being understood as justification), one was expected to give clear and regular testimony to the experience.

I affirm that there is indeed a crisis component to the work of God's sanctifying grace in the life of the believer. There is a point of entry, a recognition of God's invitation, a response "in view of God's mercy" (Rom. 12:1) that is called for and necessary on the journey toward Christlikeness. However, the emphasis upon a point of crisis that can be located in terms of date and place carries some potential, though perhaps unintended, consequences. Chief among these is the possibility that the dynamic life of holiness can become static and potentially stagnant. Stories abound of those who have been "saved and sanctified," yet the daily conduct of their lives bears little resemblance to the character of the Lord Jesus.

I will always remember one of my first meetings with a local church board as district superintendent, when I encountered a dear saint who was really causing turmoil in the life of the congregation. The atmosphere was thick with tension and anxiety as I began to address the conflicts that brought me to their meeting. We began to talk about what holiness should mean to a local church navigating differences of opinion about how things should be done.

Wanting to establish his superiority of understanding and practice, he pointed his finger in my direction and said with a scowl, "I haven't sinned in thirty years!"

I resisted the temptation to respond with, "Well, there's one!"

What I mean to illustrate with this story is the danger that overemphasis on historical testimony rather than present testimony may be part of what has created the credibility gap to which many people have responded with dismissal and disbelief. For the idea of holiness to have meaning in contemporary life, it must be understood, preached, and lived as something that truly makes a difference in the daily conduct of one's life. And this is not just about behavior. It is about holistic formation into the likeness of Jesus in a way that transforms one's life from darkness to light, from self to others, from fear to love.

There are multiple important points of theological reflection right here that are beyond the scope of this book. The point for this project is to remind us that the testimony of a holiness preacher has great importance and impact for how people come to understand God's invitation to a sanctified life. If our testimony is always transactional, imagining holiness as a date-and-place decision to consecrate ourselves fully to God, it may communicate that holiness is a once-for-all-time act that mostly involves my decision rather than God's prevenient grace. Conversely, if our testimony is always developmental and never includes decisive moments of call and response, it may communicate that holiness is more about a developing spiritual maturity than about a gift of grace that sets one into a qualitatively new journey of discipleship. I recognize that these are simplified descriptions along the dialectic of crisis versus process, but the testimony of a holiness preacher needs to communicate a call both to enter into the life of holiness and to the dynamic, present reality of the presence and power of the Spirit in one's life, forming us more and more in the character of Jesus.

One of my great concerns for the life of the church these days is the place of testimony among us. I know that our primary task is to bear witness to the world of the in-breaking kingdom of God. But there is also something important about how the community of faith itself is formed through testimony. Sacraments are foundational for this shaping, but testimony also has a shaping influence. What are the ways and where are the places in local congregations where God's people are encouraged and enabled to bear witness? Do we have purposeful opportunities for our people to share what they are coming to know of God and how God is working in their lives to do for them what the gospel promises? Pastors must lead the way in helping create an atmosphere in the congregation where this is a regular and anticipated part of life together.

I know that I grew up in the church in a different era than what we are experiencing today. There were certainly some components of the holiness church culture of the mid-twentieth century that were not healthy or theologically sound. However, I know that my life was shaped in significant and positive ways by hearing the weekly testimonies of the saints who were part of the little congregation in western Oregon that raised me in the faith. These testimonies were predictable, and we fairly knew the order in which members would rise to share their testimonies and what they would say, sometimes word for word. We could dismiss this as purely cultural and even as inwardly focused, but I am unwilling to do so. I have no doubt that the liturgy of testimony in my local church helped create in my heart and mind the space for grace-enabled confidence that I could actually know God, love God, and serve God in ways that reflected the very purposes of God in the world. It also opened the space in which I came to know and experience, in a way that changed the trajectory of my life, the sanctifying grace of God in Christ. And even more, although I would not have been able to articulate it at the time, I had a sense, even as a child, that there could be and was something holy about our life together as the people of God, the body of Christ, in that particular place and time. I learned to pray into the possibility not only of holy persons, including myself, but also of a holy church.

So, Pastor, before we think about the task or the work of preaching holiness, I want to ask you to think carefully about your own testimony. Do you have a personal testimony of the experience of entire sanctification? Does your testimony of holiness of heart and life flow naturally from your daily life in a way that inspires trust in your integrity and truthfulness as a follower of Jesus? (Having a testimony of holiness does not mean it is void of struggle, doubt, or failure.) Do you know the joy of freedom from the tyranny of sin? Can you see that your affections, desires, and attitudes have been and are being turned from a self-orientation to a self-emptying willingness to serve the other? Do you know the abiding peace and blessed assurance of the Holy Spirit in your daily life? You may have your own language for all of this, which is just fine, but don't dismiss the heart of these questions. The only way to be a faithful and effective holiness preacher is to first be living in the experience of holiness of heart and life in such a way that it does, in fact, come pouring through all of your ministry and all of your preaching.

I was raised in a wonderful Christian family and a generational Nazarene family. My great-grandfather, the Rev. A. R. Gladen, was a Methodist circuit-riding preacher in the hills of northwest Arkansas around the turn of the twentieth century. He joined up with the Nazarenes in their earliest days and was a holiness preacher for sure. He was relentless in his proclamation that there is a second definite work of grace for the believer. This was his primary criterion when my grandfather came courting his daughter. In fact, my grandfather's inability to testify to entire sanctification in those early days resulted in the Rev. Gladen withholding his blessing from the union! Through the influence of my grandmother, Olen Rowell came into the experience of entire sanctification, and there is no doubt in my mind that the story of our family was transformed as a result. As a layman, he helped to start the Church of the Nazarene congregation in which I grew up in Lebanon, Oregon. In the context of this family and local church, I came to know the graced experience of entire sanctification.

I have no memory of understanding myself as anyone other than a follower of Jesus. My earliest spiritual memories are of expressing my trust in Jesus as the forgiver of my sins and leader of my life. However, being one who by personality has a strong sense of responsibility, I soon found myself struggling to understand how I could ever measure up to what I was reading in Scripture and hearing in the testimonies of the saints about what it means to live a victorious Christian life. I confess that one of my main spiritual struggles, even to this day, can be with fear. Coming of age in the Vietnam era and in the midst of a turbulent culture, my heart and mind were regularly captured by fear, sometimes to the point of despair. (I hear these echoes today in current conversations with young people.)

Even as a young teenager, I realized that I was headed for a Christian life (there was never a doubt about whether I would follow Jesus) of uncertainty, fear, and struggle—unless God could do something for me that I was unable to do for myself. I also found myself, growing up in the age of the emerging *Playboy* culture (1960s) and having experienced a far too early exposure to pornography, needing God to reorder my mind in terms of sexuality. Combining these things with the stark truth that the culture of the holiness church was too often a culture of shame, it was a toxic recipe for a life of spiritual defeat.

I will never forget the night it came to a point of crisis. Everyone in our household had turned in for the night, but I lay awake with my mind racing, heart beating, and feeling nearly paralyzed with hopelessness and fear. Not knowing what else to do, I went in to my parents' room and awakened them, confessing my need. One of the best things my parents ever did for me happened that night. They did not impatiently tell me to get back to bed, nor did they try to minimize my struggle in order to make everything better. With gracious wisdom, they acknowledged my struggle, validated my experience, and offered their up-to-date, personal testimonies as laypeople of how God was helping them to know spiritual victory and peace. They explained that God was not only willing to forgive my sins and provide for me the hope of eternal life but that God could also fill my heart with his Holy Spirit in a way that the Spirit would purify my heart and empower me to live a Christian life day by day. They led me in a simple prayer of consecrating my life entirely to God: my past (not much of a past at that point!), my present, and my future (that was the big part). That night, kneeling beside their bed, I prayed a simple prayer of accepting God's gift of the sanctifying work of the Spirit. Nothing particularly dramatic happened. It was not highly emotional, just a confession of my faith, much in the spirit of Wesley's testimony: "I felt my heart strangely warmed." I went to bed with a new sense of peace.

The next day when I awoke, I knew that something had changed. I still am unable to describe fully how things were different, but there was an inexpressible awareness that God had done something in me that would change the trajectory of my life. I was essentially the same person, of course, but there was a brand-new sense of belonging to God and of assurance that even I had been welcomed into the fellowship of Father, Son, and Spirit in a way that would begin to renew my mind and transform my life (Rom. 12:2). I knew what Paul meant when he said, "What we have received is not the spirit of the world, but the Spirit who is from God, so that we may understand what God has freely given us" (1 Cor. 2:12). Thanks be to God!

It probably could go without saying that my Christian life since that night has not been a forty-year experience of flawless perfection or uninterrupted growth in Christ. There have been so many moments of crisis on this journey. I have known my share of struggle, doubt, and failure, but I have also known the faithful and abiding presence of Christ in such a way that crises of faith or action have not defined my discipleship but have become additional testimonies of how the sanctifying grace of God is forming me more and more in the image of Christ Jesus. What is more, I find it more than coincidental that, not long after this experience, I began to recognize an emerging awareness that God's plan for my life may be something other than my plan. Ultimately, I discovered that my full surrender to the will of God would include offering my life in service to Christ and the church as a pastor.

The risk of sharing my testimony here is offered not because I think there is anything particularly special about my story but because I want to model what I am calling for: that, as pastors, we are able and willing to open up our lives to the church and to the world in ways that become part of the preaching of the gospel. This includes the articulation of our testimony, and it especially includes the conduct of our lives.

2 THE LIFE OF A HOLINESS PREACHER

In the spirit of "practice what we preach," we also need to think soberly about how the daily conduct of our lives matches our testimony (or not). As I have written elsewhere, "The most important thing to say about pastoral life and work is something about holiness: the laying down of one's life for the sake of others."[1] I suspect all who are reading this would agree that all Christians are to reflect the self-giving life of our Lord. This responsibility is especially true, although not uniquely true, for pastors. The best biblical description of pastoral success I know is the kenotic[2] hymn of Philippians 2:

> In your relationships with one another, have the same mindset as Christ Jesus:
> Who, being in very nature God, did not consider equality with God something to be used to his own advantage;
> rather, he made himself nothing
> by taking the very nature of a servant,
> being made in human likeness.

---

1. Jeren Rowell, *Thinking, Listening, Being: A Wesleyan Pastoral Theology* (Kansas City: Beacon Hill Press of Kansas City, 2014), 85.

2. From a form of the Greek word *kenosis* that appears in Philippians 2:7. The meaning is "self-emptying" or "made nothing."

And being found in appearance as a man,
he humbled himself
by becoming obedient to death—
even death on a cross!
(Philippians 2:5–8)

For the pastor, laying down one's life in service to others is not only about meeting needs that we find in the lives of our people, though that is certainly one aspect. In this discussion, however, I am thinking especially about the way that our life among a people can become a living sign of God's transforming grace. I suspect that, having picked up this book, you were looking for resources on the particular task of preaching and teaching the biblical doctrine of sanctification. That's good, and I hope this becomes helpful to you in that way. My prior concern, however, is that pastors can get so focused on the tasks of preaching and leading our people that we can end up actually neglecting the personal and communal work of spiritual formation, particularly of being formed in the way of holiness. The first work of a pastor is to be a growing and maturing disciple of the Lord Jesus, but to do so in a uniquely public way, modeling for a people what it means to follow Jesus so thoroughly that we can join the apostle Paul in saying, "Follow my example, as I follow the example of Christ" (1 Cor. 11:1).

I have enjoyed a video interview of Dr. Walter Brueggemann, renowned biblical scholar and teacher, responding to a question about the essential pastoral task. Among his profound observations on the work of preparing to preach, Brueggemann noted that these unique disciplines "cause the pastor to live, to some extent, in a different zone. And if we are to bring a word from elsewhere, then we have to live, to some extent, elsewhere."[3] I have joined others in the argument that the lives of contemporary pastors have been so overtaken by the concerns of business and organizational management that we

---

3. Walter Brueggemann, "Preaching Moment 012: Walter Brueggemann" (St. Paul, MN: Center for Biblical Preaching, Luther Seminary, 2008), https://www.youtube.com/watch?v=J5nPlPMDDQ0.

have too often come to the essential task of preaching with less than our best energy and focus. Somewhere along the line, we succumbed to the expectation, bolstered by the modern culture of celebrity leadership, that the pastor was to be some kind of executive leadership genius, who by force of will and personality could cause the church to grow and be recognized as a desirable place to join.

I propose that what the church actually had in mind in the development of the pastoral office was that we would, under direction of the Spirit, set some people from the community of faith aside and make it possible for them to give first focus and best energies to the tasks of prayer, study of the Scriptures, and listening to God and others in ways that become life-giving in a world of noise, anxiety, and anger. This is very difficult and requires, as Brueggemann notes, enormous discipline, but this is our purpose and calling. It is only from this "elsewhere" kind of life that the pastor has any chance of calling out, under the authority of the Spirit, a covenant people that does not exist naturally in the world. Doing this requires the ability, born in prayer, for imaginative and poetic speech (to further borrow Brueggemann's language) that inspires a vision for a community of faith that actually begins to live in the world as an authentic reflection of the reign of God in Christ. The testimony of a holiness preacher is not only about preaching; it is also about the life of the preacher. This is a life that is cultivated first in the closet of prayer but then formed in the midst of life together with a people to whom the preacher has committed to be an example of what it means to live the sanctified life.

I have shared in other places that when I was being interviewed by the congregation in Shawnee, Kansas, about becoming their pastor, I was asked a fairly typical question for that kind of meeting: "What is your philosophy of ministry?" I shared a number of things in response to that question, but I have consistently remembered over the past many years what I said that night because it continued to shape how I think about my work regardless of my particular assignment. I said something like, "My first responsibility as your pastor is to be a growing, maturing disciple of Jesus Christ. And then, because of my unique role in the congregation, to allow you to see my journey and to learn something there about what it means to be a fully surrendered, sanctified, follower of Jesus." I know (and they know) that I did not do this flawlessly. However, across the years of our life together, I have no doubt that whatever influence my ministry may have had on them, it went far beyond my preaching, teaching, or administration, as important as those activities may be. They saw me live everyday life in the community, not only as a pastor but also as a husband, father, son, friend, and citizen.

Make no mistake: our people notice how we conduct our lives. They knew more than I probably thought they knew about the health of my marriage, my relationship with my children, and my reputation in the community. They saw where I went and where I didn't go. They saw what I bought and what I didn't buy. They saw how I behaved on social media and how I responded when things didn't go my way. Many pastors seem to view this glass-house existence as negative and burdensome. Well, it is, but it can also become a profound grace as we are invited to bear in our bodies the glad possibility that life can be lived under the lordship of Jesus rather than the principalities and powers of this world.

Our people not only need to *hear* biblical and theological truth about holiness; they also need to *see* how a serious Christian seeks to live it out by the grace of God. For the pastor, this is as much proclamation of the gospel as the act of preaching on Sunday. This is why I regularly reminded the pastors under my oversight that my role was not only to help them keep track of their ordination, but it was also to help them keep track of their holiness. I say this in the sense of Hebrews 13:17, which charges pastors to "have confidence in your leaders and submit to their authority, because they keep watch over you as those who must give an account." I'm talking, of course, about accountability, which is not only about spiritual oversight but also about supporting with our prayers those for whom we have shepherding responsibility. So, each year I shared with my pastors the ways that I prayed for them. I share these prayers here even as I offer them to

God on your behalf in advance of your encounter with these pages. In order to conduct your life as a faithful holiness preacher, I pray that you may have:

1. **A clear sense of calling**. I love the story in Mark 1:35–38, where Jesus responds to the expectations of people by articulating a clear vision of his mission, which keeps him from becoming sidelined trying to meet the expectations of people around him. When his disciples find him alone in prayer they say, in effect, "What are you doing out here? Don't you know the people are asking for you?" This is likely a familiar threat to every pastor. I hope we recognize how dangerous is this kind of expectation. Jesus responds by saying, "Let's go somewhere else." This response is not Jesus being unconcerned for the people; rather, it is Jesus having a clear focus on his calling as he leads the disciples "to the nearby villages—so I can preach there also" (v. 38). This ability to discern the difference between God's call and the expectations of people is essential in order for holiness preachers to remain true to our calling.

2. **Patience**. John 10:6–7 contains one of my favorite by-the-way statements that teaches us something important about the nature of leadership. After teaching on the sheep learning to hear and respond to the voice of the shepherd, John says, "Jesus told this simple story, but they had no idea what he was talking about. So he tried again" (MSG). Much of our ministry is trying again, going over old territory again and again because our people easily forget (much like ourselves). The ability to offer patience in the midst of this kind of potentially frustrating work is an ability formed in prayer as we are reminded that, like Ezekiel, we are sent to proclaim God's messages, "whether they listen or fail to listen" (Ezek. 2:5).

3. **Persistence**. This may seem redundant to the previous note, but here I am thinking more of remaining in one's assignment until there is clear direction from the Spirit to move. Acts 14 shows us Paul and others remaining in hard places and even

returning to places from which they were disinvited. This is a tenacity that is much more than personal determination. It is a Spirit-enabled resilience that holds us steady when the pressures and inevitable disappointments mount. I have long appreciated St. Benedict's addition in the sixth century of the vow of stability to the classic vows of ordination: the commitment to remain where the Spirit sends us into ministry, even and especially when it is not the place of our preference.

4. **Clarity of speech**. First Corinthians 2:1–8 and 2 Corinthians 1:12–13 are powerful correctives for us in the midst of a culture that prizes the spectacular, creative, flashy, and new. This is the commitment to proclaim the gospel with simple clarity under the power of the Holy Spirit. I like Thomas Long's response when he was asked if preaching isn't *passé* in a culture that prefers the spectacular and entertaining. Long responded by saying that he thinks people are actually hungry these days for leaders who can stand calmly, under the authority of the Spirit, and tell the truth about something. Paul writes, "My message and my preaching were not with wise and persuasive words, but with a demonstration of the Spirit's power, so that your faith might not rest on human wisdom, but on God's power" (1 Cor. 2:4–5).

5. **Wisdom**. This gift is developed over time—and lots of time, at that. It is also developed, I am sorry to say, in times of suffering. There is a grace offered in the midst of suffering faithfully that forms spiritual wisdom in us. In part, and particularly for the pastor, it is the ability to know which conversations warrant my energy and time and which need to be dismissed quickly. First Timothy 1:3–7 is the text where a young pastor is reminded by a wise mentor to avoid being dragged into trivial, useless, and divisive speech. A good word to social media users and to anyone who may be tempted to react emotionally rather than respond thoughtfully and prayerfully.

6. **Purity**. Second Timothy 2:21–22 is a powerful text that should be reviewed on a regular basis by all who dare to carry the mantle of spiritual leadership for God's people. One poor decision in a moment can shipwreck a ministry—and more. I have witnessed firsthand the devastation that can occur in a person's life, in a family, and in congregations when we pastors fail to guard our hearts and discipline the conduct of our lives through prayer and accountability. The exhortation of verse 15 is worthy of prayerful reflection: "Do your best to present yourself to God as one approved, a worker who does not need to be ashamed and who correctly handles the word of truth."

As I give myself now especially to the work of preparing "women and men to be faithful and effective ministers of the gospel of Jesus Christ,"[4] these prayers are weightier than ever in my heart. The vitality of the church depends not only upon the skill of those who guide, lead, teach, and correct but also on the vitality of our own life in Christ, our holiness. So may the Lord "equip you with everything good that you may do his will, working in us that which is pleasing in his sight, through Jesus Christ, to whom be glory forever and ever. Amen" (Heb. 13:21, ESV).

---

4. Nazarene Theological Seminary, "Mission," http://www.nts.edu/mission-and -purpose/.

P A R T   T W O

WHAT Is Holiness Preaching?

3 HOLINESS IN THE WHOLE STORY OF GOD

To preach holiness is to say something about God. The whole of the story of God as told in the Bible is a story of holiness. It is about the holy otherness of God, who is Creator and Sustainer of all. It is about holiness in God's good and beautiful creation, including us. It honestly tells the story of squandered holy love that brought distance, pain, and death into God's good creation. But it is also a story of God's absolute and holy commitment to restore God's good creation through the giving of the Son and outpouring of the Spirit; the reign of the resurrected and ascended Lord Jesus Christ over all of creation.

Preachers in the holiness tradition must keep a firm grasp of this expansive view of scriptural holiness. Otherwise, the idea of holiness can become terribly reduced to something about the disciplined conduct of one's own life. While holiness certainly does involve spiritual discipline and pietistic devotion, these can only be rightly understood as grace-enabled responses to the love of a holy God who invites us as participants in God's holiness. To preach holiness is nothing narrow or parochial. The message of holiness is not, and never has been, exclusive content for Nazarene preachers, or any other Wesleyan-Holiness preacher. It is true that the story of the Church of the Nazarene is very much a story of revival of the message of the gospel; a gospel that seeks not only to transform individual lives but also to redeem the whole world. This gospel of hope gave rise to a movement of church renewal characterized by preaching that centered on the optimistic hope of God's prevenient grace that would not only save us from our sins but also enable us to be formed in Christlikeness. This is also why Nazarenes from the beginning wisely gathered evangelism and compassion into one gospel presentation.[1]

Our message is not only preaching to the sanctification of believers. It is also the Bible truth that sanctified believers and a sanctified church do what Jesus did in the world: "proclaim good news to the poor . . . freedom for the prisoners and recovery of sight for the blind, to set the oppressed free, to proclaim the year of the Lord's favor" (Luke 4:18–19). The power of the Holiness Movement (whether in Wesley's England or nineteenth-century America) is that holiness is about a holy God who from holy love calls out, sanctifies, and forms a holy people, for the sake of announcing the reign of God in Christ to a broken world. This is the kind of holiness message that bears the seeds of our contemporary renewal. It is also why clear and compassionate holiness preaching is critical for faithful gospel ministry in our time.

The message of holiness is not something we thought up on our own a little more than a hundred years ago. It is the message of the church of Jesus Christ across twenty centuries. It is the message of God to and for the people of God for all of history. While it is certainly true that the church across these centuries sometimes lost sight of the heart of the gospel, the Spirit has nonetheless inspired, corrected, guided, and formed the people of God through desert times and through mountaintop times. The ancient message of sanctifying and transforming grace continues to resonate with a world that is hungry for the good news that in Jesus Christ, by the power of the Holy Spirit, God is at work to make all things new. A robust understanding of and ability to articulate the gospel as the whole story of God, throughout the broad sweep of the biblical narrative, is absolutely essential in order to preach holiness with passion, depth, and conviction.

---

1. I get this language from Dr. Thomas G. Nees's book *Compassion Evangelism: Meeting Human Needs* (Kansas City: Beacon Hill Press of Kansas City, 1996).

I think most pastors in the Wesleyan-Holiness space are aware of contemporary theologian N. T. Wright. The prolific work of Wright and others, who are not only doing first-rate research but also writing for the church in accessible and engaging ways, is a rich resource for the development of pastors, including the work of preaching and particularly holiness preaching. Books like *Simply Christian, Surprised by Hope, How God Became King*, and others from Wright may now be essential study for pastors who desire to preach the fullness of the gospel. Also noteworthy are the works of folks like Michael Goheen and Scot McKnight, who are among those articulating what it means to understand the gospel beyond a transactional framework of personal faith. You know others and could no doubt offer your own recommendations.

The point I want to make here is that the worst way to think of holiness preaching is to narrow our focus to certain biblical texts in an effort to bolster a doctrine, sometimes expressed in less than biblically and theologically precise language. The problem with focusing on finding certain go-to texts to preach holiness is that these texts, lifted out of the broad narrative and scope of Scripture, get reduced to biblical proofs or conversation-ending admonitions to an experience. As Diane Leclerc writes, "Biblical support for the doctrine of Holiness must be collected with great hermeneutical integrity."[2] As a young person in the church, I remember hearing the story told of a holiness preacher who allegedly declared, "Before I was sanctified, I didn't see entire sanctification anywhere in the Bible. After I was sanctified, I saw it everywhere, including places where it wasn't." This may be an apocryphal story, but perhaps it illustrates the danger of seeking to proof-text holiness.

We find the broad idea of holiness and the particular idea of sanctification throughout the biblical witness. However, to preach holiness and sanctification biblically cannot simply mean we find all the texts that use related words or ideas and exegete each text for their own

---

2. Diane Leclerc, *Discovering Christian Holiness: The Heart of Wesleyan-Holiness Theology* (Kansas City: Beacon Hill Press of Kansas City, 2010), 52.

usefulness in preaching toward holiness or an experience of entire sanctification. The careful work of exegesis must be done, of course, but something larger is needed. We need to know and be able to teach how the whole of Scripture casts the vision of a holy God and a holy people. The story of God begins with a holy God calling forth and shaping a good world that, in its beauty and flourishing, reflects the perfect fellowship of Father, Son, and Spirit. At each turn of God's creative work, the declaration is that the creation is good, good, and very good. The culminating achievement of this good creation is humanity in the image of God, sharing with God in the holy stewardship of a good and beautiful world.

This original design of God should form the foundation and beginning of all preaching and especially holiness preaching. And we need to understand how the whole of the biblical witness holds together around this vision as it is renewed at the end of the Bible. When we get to Revelation 21, we hear the glorious vision of the renewal of all creation, including humanity. The words of the risen Christ echo back through the entire story: "I am making everything new!" (v. 5). By the way, please note that the Lord does not say, "I am making all new things," as if the former things cease to exist. This distinction is important so that holiness preachers can avoid and correct the too-common message that this world will cease to exist and that we will have eternal life in some kind of new place called *heaven* that is often described in fairly disembodied ways. We preach the gospel of the risen Lord Jesus Christ. We believe in the resurrection of the body. We believe in the redemption of all things. The eighth chapter of Romans is a text to which holiness preachers often turn. However, keep the whole chapter in view and make sure to include the part about the redemption of creation itself (vv. 19–25)! If we only begin from Genesis 3 forward, starting with the fractured relationship between God and humanity, or frame holiness simply as trying to behave right here so that someday we can go to heaven, then the idea of holiness struggles to find its rich basis in the love and character of God and in God's original design for a flourishing world.

With this said, we can and should begin to look at how the components (genres) of the Bible speak uniquely to holiness and form an essential part of a holistic understanding of holiness. The Old Testament is all about a holy God calling forth a holy people. We have already noted that the story begins with the creation of a world in which God and humanity enjoy a pure relationship of holy love. But then we get to Genesis 3, and under the consequences of self-oriented rebellion, humanity is unable to restore that which was lost in the misuse of freedom. Thus launches the entire story of our redemption, of God's initiating movement toward us that calls us forth from darkness into the light of God's holy love. Part of that movement, we must tell the truth, includes God's judgment of our sin through discipline. This is not a retributive discipline from an angry God but the prodigal love of a Father, who "gave them over" (Rom. 1:24) in order that they might "come to [their] senses" and return home (Luke 15:17).

From the place of judgment, God keeps calling humanity—through Noah, Abraham, Isaac, Jacob, and onward through the story—into covenant with God's self. God's desire for the fruit of God's creative love is that we would be holy, giving articulation to perhaps the most essential holiness text of the Bible: "Be holy because I, the LORD your God, am holy" (Lev. 19:2). In the Old Testament, the idea of God's holiness being reflected in humanity is nearly always a corporate vision; the idea that the people of God in their life together would image the holy character of God. We began by noting that to speak of holiness is to speak of God. Yet it is clear in the Bible story that by faith, through a trusting relationship with God, the people of God can become holy. Most essentially this means that things and people who are made holy can be considered to be holy when they fulfill the holy purpose for which they were created. This involves cleansing and setting apart, the acts of a holy God, but it also involves consecration and obedience, the grace-enabled acts of a responsive people.

In terms of the particular genres of the Bible and how its books uniquely speak the message of holiness, let us consider a broad sweep of the books of the Old and New Testaments and how they might be heard in terms of the overarching message of holiness.

First, in the Pentateuch (comprised of Genesis, Exodus, Leviticus, Numbers, and Deuteronomy), we get the story of God's creative design, as we have noted, but then the fascinating story begins to unfold of a holy God's relationship with an all-too-often unholy people. One of the important ways of describing holiness comes into view in these texts with holiness as fidelity and covenant love. Particularly in Exodus, we hear the story of a God who will stop at almost nothing to rescue a lost and broken people. Leviticus and Deuteronomy give us different yet complementary visions of what it means to be a holy people. Dr. Timothy Green's book *The God Plot* lays this out in engaging fashion, and my simple summary will not do the work justice. I commend his book for careful study as a resource to help us recapture the rhetorical function of these texts.[3] Let it simply be noted in this context that Old Testament narratives reflect the work of two distinct voices: the *prophetic* voice and the *priestly* voice. Both of these voices or perspectives need to be heard as we study Old Testament texts.

"The prophetic voice paints an engaging portrait of the gracious entry door opened by God so that his people might actively join him in his divine plot."[4] Here are the compelling stories of God as deliverer of God's people, as provider, and as covenant maker. This voice is singing the song of amazing grace and of a God who is always working to bring his people back into the unashamed relationship into which we were created.

The priestly voice, singing harmony with the prophetic voice, certainly resonates with the grace-filled invitation to wholeness, and it also strikes the chords of cleansing and purity. Here the call is to

---

3. With this language and idea, I am reaching to Thomas G. Long, *Preaching and the Literary Forms of the Bible* (Philadelphia: Fortress Press, 1989).

4. Timothy Green, *The God Plot: Living with Holy Imagination* (Kansas City: Beacon Hill Press of Kansas City, 2014), 34.

"unadulterated devotion" and concern for an "untainted heart, in relationship to the Lord."[5]

In all of this rich, honest, messy, and beautiful telling of God's story of relationship with God's people, holiness is presented as the grace-enabled ways in which "the covenant community functions as the glory bearer in the world."[6] This is our invitation and assignment as God's people, that our lives, and especially our life together, would be an authentic reflection of God's glory, the glory revealed in the Son, our Lord Jesus Christ. Therefore, to be a holy people is not to stand apart from the world and practice doing holy things in isolation. If we only hear the priestly voice, we could get this image. But the fullness of the text invites us to holiness that participates with God in mission to the world, a mission that delivers, releases, restores, and signals hope in God's renewal of all things.

The Prophets (Isaiah, Jeremiah, Daniel, and the so-called minor prophets) are all part of this song as well, of course. Isaiah, coming onto the stage at one of the worst moments in Israel's history, receives his call and commission in a powerful scene of God's majestic holiness, yet there is also a clear articulation of God's missionary concern for God's people and the hope-filled imagination of salvation and restoration. Isaiah's vision is for the redemption of God's people where all that is broken is healed and "streams in the desert" (Isa. 35:6) begin to make the parched land alive again. The invitation is to join the journey on this highway of new life that is called the "Way of Holiness" (v. 8), where those whom God has redeemed will walk with joy. In other words, where Old Testament texts often seem to be viewed as imaging a holiness that is about legalistic obedience to the law of God, the texts are rich with the hopeful promise of God's mission to restore and renew God's good creation—and even more, that God is inviting God's covenant people to join in this journey toward the new Jerusalem.

---

5. Ibid., 124.
6. Ibid., 138.

We also have to acknowledge and faithfully preach the word of judgment that is clearly a part of prophetic speech, usually because the people of God are ignoring their call to be a holy people in a way that brings justice within their communities and to their neighbors. This is not only a historical note—it is also a continued word of correction to the contemporary church, particularly a holiness church that too often has forsaken its moorings in holiness as social justice. Personal holiness and social holiness are not in opposition but form, in their dynamic relationship, a balanced and holistic understanding and practice of holy living. The quintessential call of God in this regard is the well-known exhortation of the prophet Micah: "He has shown you, O mortal, what is good. And what does the LORD require of you? To act justly and to love mercy and to walk humbly with your God" (6:8).

The Wisdom Literature of the Old Testament is another rich resource for preaching holiness. This section is an oft-neglected genre of Scripture for holiness preaching, perhaps because sapiential literature (Job, Psalms, Proverbs, Song of Songs, Ecclesiastes) works largely in affective rather than propositional ways. The focus is on the pursuit of wisdom that is carried in poetic speech, rather than the work of epistemology carried in rational sequencing (logic, proposition, and argument). The neglect of Wisdom Literature for preaching holiness may reveal that we tend to think of holiness preaching in terms of doctrine rather than in terms of relational intimacy.

Psalm 15 is a beautiful example of how wisdom speaks to God's call toward and provision for holiness of heart and life. The psalmist asks: "LORD, who may dwell in your sacred tent? Who may live on your holy mountain?" (v. 1). And the answer comes back: "The one whose walk is blameless, who does what is righteous, who speaks the truth from their heart" (v. 2)—and it goes on with this lofty description of those who are acceptable in the presence of God. At first, hearing this may seem discouraging and hopeless. Who among us is blameless?

This word came to a people who could easily rely on a religious system. It was not unusual for them to reduce what God intended as covenant relationship to a system of laws, sacrifices, and rituals.

In this way of thinking, the temptation may be to think that if one adheres to the system and follows the rules, then one is welcomed into the presence of God. This word comes to remind God's people that their salvation is not based on their ability to act like religious people but is, in fact, much deeper. As they stand at the entrance of the temple, they need to see not their self-justification but their need of forgiveness and grace. The question was not, "Have you fulfilled the requirements of your religion?" The question was, "Do you live out of the covenant? Is Yahweh Lord of the everyday?"

The same essential temptation potentially confronts followers of Jesus. In the invitation to a holy life, is God simply laying upon us another and more intense legalism? Or do we hear in God's initiating movement toward us, from the establishing of Israel to the birth of the church, the hope-filled message that God is able to do something in us, for us, and through us to form in us the very holiness that God's holy love requires? Psalms as a holiness text is a helpful way of preaching the Psalter because these texts are so visceral and honest. They not only express faith, they also express doubt, anger, and fear—but within the safety of confidence in a God who is working to redeem a broken world.

While it is not possible here to survey fully how Old Testament genres might resource holiness preaching, I hope these few notes might expand our biblical horizon to the whole story of God as nearly limitless material from which to proclaim God's gift of sanctifying grace. Helpful examples can be found in several works, but I would note especially some essays that are gathered in the book *Biblical Resources for Holiness Preaching: From Text to Sermon*, by H. Ray Dunning and Neil B. Wiseman.

When we come to the New Testament, holiness as a communal ideal and experience continues, yet we begin to see also the personal (though never private) dimensions of graced response to the God who not only calls us to be holy but, in Christ, is the way of holiness. Here a holy life begins to be described in terms of purity or cleansing, which is different from, although certainly related to, pious behaviors that may be listed as rules for holy living. I remember Dr. William Greathouse joking that he wanted to get a trainload of Avis buttons for Nazarenes to wear. Avis is an American rental car company whose marketing slogan used to be "We try harder."

Our temptation as holiness people has been to understand holiness as something we achieve through our disciplined efforts. The essence of the purity to which the New Testament calls us is the gift of God in Christ that comes through the cleansing work of the Spirit. It is also described in terms of fulfilling one's purpose (telios) or, as typically translated, "maturity" or "perfection." The term perfection is challenging in contemporary Western contexts because it suggests flawlessness, or one's arrival to the ultimate ideal. Therefore, part of the task of the holiness preacher is to define biblical terms and teach our people what it truly means to speak of the telios that can be experienced through the work of entire (meaning all, not finished) sanctification.

There is no doubt in the New Testament that holiness is about the whole person: heart, mind, soul, and strength. It also has in focus the community, the body of Christ, as well as individual Christians. Many of the New Testament texts that tend to be read and preached personally are actually meant to speak to the community of faith as a whole. A great example of this is noted by Dr. Tom Noble in his observation on 1 Thessalonians 5:23, a text often quoted in support of the entire sanctification of individual believers. He says that in the Greek text of this verse, the word translated "entirely" (NRSV) is not an adverb modifying "sanctify" but an adjective modifying a plural "you," meaning the people of God.[7] So when Paul writes, "May the God of peace himself sanctify you entirely" (NRSV), he is expressing his prayer that the community of faith may be sanctified—that is, set apart for the holy purposes of God in the world.

This interpretation would be in keeping with the prayer of our Lord as recorded in John 17, when Jesus prays that we, the people of God,

---

7. T. A. Noble, Holy Trinity: Holy People: The Theology of Christian Perfecting (Eugene, OR: Cascade Books, 2013), 35.

would live together in the unity of the Spirit, that we might so reflect the perfect love of God "that the world may believe" (v. 21, NRSV). As Kenneth Waters suggests, holiness is "more than a character trait or virtue. It is also human response to the needs of others. Holiness is both inward and outward."[8] Waters also notes that New Testament holiness is both holistic and singular. That is, holiness is not simply one virtue among a set of desired virtues in the life of the believer (although it is sometimes singled out in the listing of Christian virtue)—instead, it is more adequately viewed as foundational to all virtues. Perhaps another way to say it is that holiness gathers all Christian virtue into a cohesive expression of Christlike bearing and behavior.

Another important point of complexity in the New Testament description of holiness is that sanctification is presented as the whole of God's project in the lives of believers and in the community of faith, but it is also presented as episodic and decisive. Theologically, we speak of this in terms of sanctification as a description of the entirety of what God means to do in the restoration, reconciliation, and redemption of our lives in Christ by the work of the Holy Spirit. However, we also speak of *initial* sanctification that is initiated by grace, through faith in the Lord Jesus Christ, which comes when one confesses faith in the Lord Jesus as Savior. Understanding this point helps keep us from the faulty idea that we only receive the Holy Spirit in a second work of grace. From initial sanctification we can then speak of growth in grace, or *progressive* sanctification, by which one is formed more and more into the image of Christ Jesus until one comes to experience the grace of *entire* sanctification by which we are transformed by the infilling of the Holy Spirit, freeing us from the tyranny of sin and empowering us to live the life of Jesus in the world. This is not to suggest that we have arrived in some way; progressive sanctification continues throughout our lives until we come to *final* sanctification,

---

8. Kenneth L. Waters Sr., "Holiness in New Testament Perspective" in *The Holiness Manifesto*, ed. Kevin W. Mannoia and Don Thorsen (Grand Rapids: William B. Eerdmans Publishing Company, 2008), 41.

or glorification—when, in death, we are removed from the presence of sin. As Dr. Leclerc notes, "Sanctification . . . refers to the how of holiness."[9] In one sense, although we rightly speak of conversion and sanctification as moments of response to the grace of God, we can also be comfortable to speak of being converted and being sanctified within the dynamic vitality of life in Christ.

Planning to preach on holiness tends to move the preacher quickly toward the Epistles, particularly Paul's letters, because there we encounter the most familiar language of holiness theology. These are certainly important texts, but as David Kendall observes, "Holiness preaching and teaching seldom visit the Gospels."[10] He further notes, "Jesus had little to say about holiness,"[11] which stands to reason in that Jesus is not formulating or teaching a doctrine. Jesus is the "image of the invisible God" (Col. 1:15); he is holiness. Therefore, we need to lean into the life and teaching of Jesus, not in some kind of moralistic way to define a list of rules for holy living. Rather, we need to capture the very heart of Jesus, the character of the One who makes known to us the Father's heart (see John 1:18, NRSV). For this reason, holiness preaching ought to find its moorings in the life and teaching of Jesus as told in the Gospels. Kent Brower's fine work, Holiness in the Gospels, is a tremendous help here. As Dr. Brower writes, "Holiness teaching is rooted in the incarnation of Christ."[12] Therefore, the Gospels will be at the center of holiness preaching.

Chief among these texts is what we have come to call the Sermon on the Mount (Matt. 5:1–7:29). As a new pastor, I spent the first several weeks of my ministry at Shawnee Church of the Nazarene in Shawnee, Kansas, preaching through the Sermon on the Mount under the title "Holiness as Jesus Taught It." In two subsequent interim as-

9. Leclerc, Discovering Christian Holiness, 48.

10. David W. Kendall, "Jesus and a Gospel of Holiness" in The Holiness Manifesto, 57.

11. Ibid., 58.

12. Kent Brower, Holiness in the Gospels (Kansas City: Beacon Hill Press of Kansas City, 2005), 18.

signments, I gave the first several weeks of those opportunities to the same preaching and found the congregational conversations that grew from those sermons to be fruitful in terms of the spiritual growth of individuals, and formational in terms of the ethos of the community of faith. The preaching of Jesus is a compelling and attractive call to holiness of heart and life. The watershed text is Matthew 5:48: "Be perfect, therefore, as your heavenly Father is perfect." This would be a terrifying and disheartening expectation from the mouth of our Lord, unless we understand rightly, and help our people to understand rightly, that what seems an impossible expectation is actually a grace-filled invitation to a holy life. This is the work and privilege of a good and godly holiness preacher.

There are many pericopes in the Gospels, of course, from which the call to holiness can be preached. Much of what we find in the Gospels is Jesus confronting the legalism and rigidity of religion and offering a way of loving and serving God that is rooted in mercy and love. This theme, in itself, is a firm foundation from which to preach a way of holy living that resembles Jesus rather than fearful conservatism or fearful liberalism. The pastoral challenge of these texts is that contemporary Christians often read the attitudes and actions of Pharisees as something distant from their own experience. I have often said to my people something like, "Whenever we read 'Pharisees' in the Gospels, we can just go ahead and substitute our own names." We can and should find ourselves in the Gospel stories, and usually, if we are doing it right, we will find ourselves under scandalous confrontation similar to that which offended the religious professionals of Jesus's day. But this confrontation is not for its own sake; rather, it is to invite us and compel us into the way of love that, when lived with our whole hearts, transforms our lives, the community of faith, and the world.

The Acts of the Apostles (combined with Luke) would clearly be an important text for the preaching of holiness. Luke gives us the story of the fulfillment of the Pentecostal promise, and it is clear that we witness in the disciples the baptism with the Holy Spirit to which

John pointed when he announced the arrival of the one "whose sandals I am not worthy to untie" (John 1:27). My own point of caution in preaching from Acts is that we be careful not to force the narrative into the logic of two works of grace in a way that seeks to solve and even minimize the fluid and dynamic nature of the work of the Spirit in the infant church. The story of the Holy Spirit sending (sometimes pushing) the church of Jesus into the world on mission is a compelling source from which to proclaim the continuing work of the Spirit in the missional sending of a holy church into the world for the holy purposes of God.

The Pauline Epistles obviously provide a tremendous source for holiness preaching. At the center of these texts is the letter to the Romans, from which so much of what we know as holiness theology and preaching arises. Romans has played an important role in the life of the church and particularly the Holiness Movement. As Dr. Leclerc notes in Discovering Christian Holiness, Martin Luther's understanding of the gospel was transformed through careful reading and reflection on Romans. And John Wesley's life was changed, sparked by the hearing of Luther's preface to Romans. Chapters 6 through 8 of Romans give the heart of the call to and provision for a holy life. And chapter 12 is rich with instruction and admonition toward a life of holiness. There really is no exhausting of textual resources in these few chapters for the prayerful and thoughtful preacher who goes to the text in loving service to a congregation whom she or he loves and desires to offer the hope-filled gospel of holiness of heart and life.

The general Epistles also provide tremendous resources for preaching holiness. First Peter, for example, is a beautiful and relevant exhortation for the contemporary church seeking to finds its way in a time of dislocation and uncertainty. In 1 Peter, we are reminded of the core exhortation to holiness from Leviticus: "Be holy, because I am holy" (1 Pet. 1:16; cf. Lev. 11:44, 45; 19:2). We hear in 1 Peter a strong and decisive call to followers of Jesus not only toward holiness in their own lives but also that together they might be a holy church, "living stones," a "spiritual house," a "holy priesthood" (2:5). And in what I judge to be one of the strongest holiness texts in the Epistles, 1 Peter 3:15 says, "But in your hearts sanctify Christ as Lord. Always be ready to make your defense to anyone who demands from you an accounting for the hope that is in you" (NRSV). This call comes in the midst of a profound discussion on the reality of suffering that Christ followers will likely experience in the world, yet this suffering is being redeemed by the power of the Spirit to proclaim the gospel.

In a similar way, John's Apocalypse (Revelation) can and should be taken back from narrow and misguided interpretive efforts to map out the end of the world. The letter was intended as a word of encouragement, strength, and revival to a church that was wrestling with the temptation to become enmeshed in the values and priorities of empire, rather than remembering its true identity as citizens of a new heaven and new earth that is both now and not yet, inaugurated in the coming of our Lord Jesus and culminated in his coming again. This is a timely word to the contemporary church of Jesus Christ as we seek to find our voice in the midst of changed and changing cultures. The gospel of holiness should strengthen our people for such a time as this. It seems that the church has, in many ways, become anxious and afraid, mirroring the anxiety of the world. The truth of the gospel is that we need not fear because we are able, under the power of the Spirit, to go forth in service to the world in Jesus's name with grace and with peace. Holiness preaching is missional preaching that finds its voice in hope rather than in fear.

One final note, to say something about the letter to the Hebrews. Although Hebrews is a complex and challenging book from which to preach, exegetical and homiletical work in Hebrews can be rewarding. The theme of Hebrews, written to Jewish Christians, is to establish Jesus Christ as the final and supreme offering of God's self to the world. Finding its voice in positive contrasts to the Levitical system, Hebrews presents a positive picture of purity as the basis for sanctification—a purity that is not only external and ritual but also internal and real. One of the leading texts of the Holiness Movement comes from Hebrews: "Make every effort to live in peace with everyone and to be holy; without holiness no one will see the Lord" (12:14). Although this text has sometimes been misused to suggest that one is in danger of "missing heaven" without a second work of grace, it does nonetheless come in the midst of a call to fix "our eyes on Jesus, the pioneer and perfecter of faith" (v. 2). With this important christological focal point, Hebrews provides the careful pastor with meaningful material from which to proclaim God's full provision for us in Christ Jesus.

While this is obviously a cursory review of holiness in the whole of the story of God, I hope it helps us remember that to preach holiness is not to reach only to certain texts in support of an expressed doctrine. Holiness preaching should always locate the message of heart holiness and the provision of God's sanctifying grace within the whole scope of God's redemptive work in Jesus, by the presence and power of the Holy Spirit.

4 TEXTUAL RESOURCES FOR PREACHING HOLINESS

Having surveyed holiness in the broad scope of the biblical witness in the previous chapter, here I would like to offer preachers some specific direction or ideas about how certain key texts might be approached for preaching holiness. This is certainly not intended as a comprehensive overview but only to spark your own prayerful thinking about how some of the central texts of holiness could be preached in the context of congregational life.

From the recognition that holiness is centered in Jesus, let us begin with the Gospels. As previously noted, Kent Brower's *Holiness in the Gospels* is a must-read for holiness preachers. As Brower notes, the Gospels not only narrate the historical life of Jesus of Nazareth but also "are theological documents."[1] They not only tell the stories of the disciples' encounters with Jesus, but they also mean to inspire faith. As John puts it, "These are written so that you may come to believe that Jesus is the Messiah, the Son of God, and that through believing you may have life in his name" (20:31, NRSV).

Brower traces the preaching of holiness in the Gospels from the backdrop of the Jewish cultural and religious milieu. As we know, Jesus stepped into a religious world filled with developed expectations of what it meant to worship a holy God and be a holy people. In the

---

1. Brower, *Holiness in the Gospels*, 16.

tensions and confrontations we see in the Gospels between Jesus and the religious professionals, we are invited to consider that holiness may be much more than strict adherence to the law and ritual purity. In Jesus, we see that holiness finds its life and power in love, and this love that flows from the heart of God moves toward the sinful and broken world rather than away from it. Dr. Brower writes, "God is not a finger-wagging, fussy, and stern patriarch who watches vigilantly lest someone break a rule. Rather, His holiness is His essential character, shown as a gracious and loving God, slow to anger and plenteous in mercy."[2] Thanks be to God!

For Matthew, Jesus comes announcing the arrival of the kingdom of God and, in response to this good news, invites us to come into the reign of God, which is expressed in a life that is totally devoted to loving God holistically (heart, mind, soul, strength). But even this is not the end of it because this kind of wholehearted love for God finds its necessary expression in loving our neighbor even as we would love and care for ourselves. This is the "righteousness [that] surpasses that of the Pharisees and the teachers of the law" (Matt. 5:20) because it flows not from obligation or religion but from love.

A central text in Matthew from which a robust understanding of holiness can be preached is, of course, what we have come to call the Sermon on the Mount. This text is usually framed as Matthew 5:1–7:29. However, as Brower notes, the language of 4:23 "forms an inclusio with 9:35."[3] In other words, Matthew, with theological intention, bookends the sermon with the gospel word that "Jesus went throughout Galilee, teaching in their synagogues and proclaiming the good news of the kingdom and curing every disease and every sickness among the people" (4:23, NRSV). This signals us to understand the Sermon on the Mount not as a listing of virtues or behaviors to locate us into the way of holiness but as a portrait of the work of the

2. Ibid., 55.
3. Ibid., 111.

Spirit in one's life, from which is brought forth the good fruit of the kingdom of God.

At the risk of limiting rather than sparking imagination, then, let me offer one possibility for structuring a series of sermons on the Matthew texts we are discussing. I gathered these sermons under the general title "Holiness as Jesus Taught It."[4] One way to preach these sermons is successively across eighteen weeks. I recommend this approach during what is typically called Ordinary Time in the Christian year. On one occasion, I preached these messages in three successive Lenten seasons, departing from Lectionary texts in order to do so. My practice reveals that, although I have great appreciation for and often follow Lectionary texts for preaching, I also believe that sometimes pastoral discernment may move us toward different structures. The following is an annotated outline of this series of messages that were preached in order to bring congregations into an encounter with a holy God who desires, calls forth, and enables a holy people.

Matthew 5: Holiness as Jesus Taught It

Text: Matthew 5:1–12
Sermon Title: It's in the Attitude

The familiar Beatitudes, if truly heard, begin to call into question our typical understanding of what makes for a blessed life. Qualities like poor, mournful, meek, and hungry do not sound like a recipe for a happy life—unless, that is, God is able to turn them from curses to blessings as we learn to live into the ways of the reign of God rather than the ways of the world. Beatitudes are ways of being, not ways of acting. Holiness works from the inside out, not the other way around, and transforms how we think about blessing, success, and even happiness.

---

4. Some of these ideas and corresponding language were worked out in collaboration with my friend David Busic, with whom I had the joy of sharing parish ministry in the early 1990s.

Text: Matthew 5:13–16
Sermon Title: Be What You Are

Before Jesus gives any command to do something, he tells us who we are: the salt of the earth and the light of the world. Again, *being* precedes *doing*. The primary images of salt and light remind us that the value of these essential life resources rises from their nature—their character, if you will. "Holiness of heart and life" is language that gets the order right. Holiness is rooted in a heart transformed by God's perfect love and then expressed in a life of love.

Text: Matthew 5:17–20
Sermon Title: How Good Do You Have to Be?

What does it mean for our righteousness to surpass that of religious professionals? How good does one have to be? Better than we can be. And right there is where real discipleship begins. Holiness is not conformity to the law but the gift of sanctification that purifies our hearts and enables us to live a holy life in grateful response to the transforming work of God in Christ.

Text: Matthew 5:21–26
Sermon Title: The Ugly Truth about Anger

The ugly truth about anger is that it so easily gives way to sin. It can quickly turn to choices that are in no way consistent with life in the kingdom of God. The profound idea here is that in the life of holiness even basic, seemingly instinctual emotions like anger are brought under the lordship of Jesus Christ. Religious people think they can justify their holiness if they avoid murder, adultery, and the like, but Jesus presses the heart of holiness much deeper. Jesus wants to examine things like anger, hatred, and lust—the kinds of things that can be hidden in a religious life but must be cleansed in a holy life.

Text: Matthew 5:27–30
Sermon Title: A Call to Sexual Purity

In the midst of what some have called a pornographic age, this text calls for particular attention on the part of a people who are being sanctified. The key question here may be, *Are you willing to take even drastic measures in order to honor God and to be pure in the conduct of life?* It should be clear, by this point in this book, that this is certainly not a call simply to moral purity or behavior alone as the heart of a holy life. However, holiness of heart and life does call for discipline. The hyperbolic advice of Jesus here is a sobering call to us in a time when moral and ethical compromise are the order of the day.

Text: Matthew 5:31–37
Sermon Title: Truth Speakers and Promise Keepers

Could holiness have anything to do with telling the truth? Jesus is speaking to some folks who have learned to manipulate the concept of truth-speaking in order to fit it comfortably into a self-serving agenda. The practice of oaths has become a morass of technical loopholes that people think they can use to avoid transparent relationship. Jesus wants to give us the freedom to live such a simple, honest life that in our speech and in our dealings with people, our yes can simply mean yes and our no can simply mean no.

Text: Matthew 5:38–48
Sermon Title: When Love Hurts

The preacher may be tempted here to rush right to the troubling word of verse 48. However, locating Jesus's words about perfection in the context of real-life conversation about enemies and retaliation gives it a practicality that may assist us to hear properly Jesus's watershed exhortation. When temptation comes for retaliation, when the opportunity arises for vengeance, when no one in the world would blame you for getting even, Jesus says the Christian goes another way. Going another way is impossible, unless God is able to do something in us and for us that we cannot do for ourselves. Herein is the power of the call to "be perfect." It is not about perfect performance but about perfect love—and this not of ourselves but the gift of God. It is not a love that we manufacture in our own hearts. It is God's love that is given to us that now we are called on to share with those around us. It is treating others the same way that God has treated us. It is holiness.

Matthew 6: The Marks of the True Disciple

Text: Matthew 6:1–4
Sermon Title: Quiet Service

Jesus sets one of the critical marks of a true Christian as quiet service: acts of self-giving love that no one but God may ever know about. We see here one group of folks who do the right things outwardly, yet they are condemned. There is another group who also do the right things with the right heart, and they are rewarded. The difference centers on motive. Why do we do what we do? The exhortation of our Lord here is not to be involved in acts of righteousness; the assumption is that we *are* involved in these things. The challenge here is to be careful about our hearts, which we are enabled to do by God's sanctifying grace.

Text: Matthew 6:5–13
Sermon Title: Genuine Prayer

Prayer is at the center; it is the very heart of a holy life. There are two things Jesus says must be avoided in genuine prayer: one is praying to impress others, and the other is praying to impress God. In both cases we forget whom we are talking to. Genuine prayer is not a matter of getting the words right. It is a matter of the heart being so open and honest before the Lord that we see God and see God's power to make us true followers of the Son. The kind of in-your-closet prayer that Jesus is speaking of here is the place where holiness of heart and life is shaped most of all.

Text: Matthew 6:9–15
Sermon Title: Active Forgiveness

Jesus knows that with a spirit of unforgiveness lurking in our hearts, everything else he is talking about in the Sermon on the Mount will unravel. None of it works if we refuse to live in reconciliation and peace with each other. This is the heart of the gospel. Too often we say we offer forgiveness, and then the practical strategy is simply to avoid the other. This is not what Jesus has in mind. Christian forgiveness is refusing to let anything permanently destroy the relationship. Forgiveness is what distinguishes authentic Christian faith from religion. It is also a major part of what enables us to understand that holiness is never a private matter; it always has in view a holy people who live together as a sign of God's in-breaking kingdom.

Text: Matthew 6:16–18
Sermon Title: Self-Denial

Jesus knew that in the world we are seduced and distracted every day by that which is offered for our happiness, pleasure, and comfort. In a world of plenty and a culture of excess, a holy life is formed significantly through learning the spiritual discipline of self-denial. It is a way of remembering that we depend on God alone and draw all our strength and resource from God. We fast to listen to God. We fast to remember our dependency, and we fast to be sustained only by God. The promise of Jesus is, "Your Father, who sees what is done in secret, will reward you" (v. 18).

Text: Matthew 6:19–24
Sermon Title: Straight Priorities

A major challenge to our holiness is that many of us in the Western world live in cultures that are choking to death on our excesses. Having our priorities straight is fundamentally a matter of the heart. This is the essence of the entire Sermon on the Mount. Holiness is an inward reality that results in an outward life that reflects the character of Jesus. This connects to Jesus's words in the text about our eyes. Being a person of light is a matter of how we see. Having good eyes means that our hearts are uncluttered and our priorities are straight. We know who we are, we know whose we are, and we know what finally matters in life.

Text: Matthew 6:25–34
Sermon Title: Trustful Rest

There is a marked difference between a life fully devoted to God and the rather mindless preoccupation that seems so characteristic of life in our world. The busyness of our lives is the enemy of genuine discipleship. The kind of life into which Jesus is calling us requires practices of silence, solitude, and, most of all, a quiet heart. Practicing these things seems counterintuitive in a world that bases value on productivity and acquisition. Jesus teaches that the alternative to anxiety over what we do not control is to release our grasp of that which we do control.

Matthew 7: The Outward Life of a Disciple

Text: Matthew 7:1–6
Sermon Title: What Goes around . . .

In this well-known and oft-quoted text, Jesus is not giving a new rule to follow about being nice to people. And he is saying a lot more than "mind your own business." Jesus is talking about being a person whose heart has been captivated by the mercy of God. When one lives in the awareness of God's mercy toward us, the appropriate response is to return the mercy in your attitude and action toward others. Jesus knows that in order to make ourselves look better, or simply feel better, we become experts in criticism. So Jesus invites us into a different way. The way of holiness is a graced way that transforms our relationships with one another "in view of God's mercy" (Rom. 12:1).

Text: Matthew 7:7–12
Sermon Title: Trust the Giver

After calling us to this amazing life of grace, forgiveness, and righteousness—after nearly three chapters of the loftiest kind of vision of what it means to be a true disciple—Jesus now asks, "Do you want this? Ask and you will receive. Do you desire to live a life that is totally acceptable to God? Seek it and you will find it. Do you want to be pleasing to the Father? Knock and it will be opened up to you." Is this true? Will God truly give us everything we need to live the life that God's holiness demands? Can we really know the joyful life that holiness provides? Jesus is saying that the life of holiness is available for the asking, but we have to trust the character of the Giver. Jesus's words are not a ready-made prescription for serving our own interests. This is an offer to live the kind of life to which he is calling us, not by our own ability but by his grace.

Text: Matthew 7:13–14
Sermon Title: Becoming Narrow

This familiar text is likely understood by many Christians as having to do with discipline and effort. It is the idea that taking the narrow way is a matter of our work and how serious we may be about the way of Jesus. There is no way to hear Jesus's sermon without knowing that discipline is indeed part of the way of holiness. However, we must keep clear that spiritual discipline is always the grace-enabled response to what God is doing to redeem us and the world in which we live. The narrow road is not about our tenacious ability always to do the right thing. The narrow road journey is about taking the path of grace instead of self-effort; about trusting God to remake us from the inside out.

Text: Matthew 7:15–23
Sermon Title: Good Fruit

The words of warning that now come into Jesus's sermon come on two fronts. One is the idea of being careful about false prophets, or spiritual leaders who are faking it—because of the tremendous damage they can do. The other is the idea of being careful that you are not counted among the false prophets as one of them. It is certainly possible to try and walk the way of Jesus simply by looking the part, though that will soon lead to disaster. The life of holiness to which Jesus calls us is first an inner work of the Spirit that then produces the fruit of righteousness in terms of loving and serving our neighbors. This way of talking of "good fruit" reminds us of Paul's description of the fruit of the Spirit in Galatians, which is a unified, holistic description of the character qualities that are formed in a person who is fully surrendered to the lordship of Jesus.

Text: Matthew 7:24–29
Sermon Title: Talk Is Cheap

This familiar Sunday school text is certainly much more than a cute moral lesson. It is a life-changing call to a radical style of discipleship. Now, having heard this amazing Sermon on the Mount, we have two possibilities from which to choose. There are some who will hear this truth and perhaps seem like they are building their life upon it, but in the end the truth hasn't gone any deeper than the external. This person is likely to be washed out when trouble comes. The other choice is to respond to Jesus's teaching by allowing it to sink deeply into the bedrock of one's life so that it not only reforms the external but first transforms the heart and core of one's life. It is possible to go through life and have the holiness externals down. But there is coming a day—a storm day, a test day—when the real substance of what we are in Christ is revealed. It is about foundations. Jesus asks, "Rock or sand?"

Again, this summative outline of sermons from Matthew's Gospel is intended only to be illustrative of the opportunities we have to preach holiness from the richness of Jesus's life, ministry, and teaching as told to us in the Gospels. This focal point will help our exhortations to holiness to find their character first in the love of God in Christ and then in disciplines and patterns of holy living that arise in grateful response to God's love. I've said nothing of the uniqueness of Johannine literature but would also urge the cultivation of these beautiful texts, including the epistle texts that bear John's name, as a rich resource for preaching holiness.

Under the goal of providing practical resources for pastors and preachers, I will turn now to some ideas for approaching preaching holiness from Paul's letter to the Romans. Many have characterized Romans as the apostle's *summa theological*, or most sophisticated, systematic theological discourse. This may be true, but I also find Romans to be pastoral in the best sense. That is, it seeks to place the conduct of Christians in the world on the foundation of a theological orientation that is defined and shaped by the gospel.

Among the ways we might locate the occasion of this letter, certainly a major part is helping the Christian congregations in Rome to navigate their cultural challenges, both in terms of empire and in terms of the unity of the church as Jews and gentiles come together. What will secure the vitality of Rome's Christian witness must go much deeper than social agreements about how to get on with each other and with pagan neighbors. The church must find its strength in the power of the gospel, which will enable them to resist conforming to the ways of the world and, instead, be transformed by the "renewing of your mind" (Rom. 12:2) in Christ Jesus. Contemporary preaching is in desperate need of expanding its perspective far above the pragmatic interests of how to be happy, successful, or even good. Romans lifts our vision to the grand vista of God's redemptive love expressed and offered to the world in the person and work of Jesus Christ.

Therefore, it is important for the pastoral preacher to have what I call a conversational overview of the scope and sequence of Paul's letter. I mean by this that, in order to bring hermeneutical integrity to the exegesis and proclamation of these texts, one must have a strong sense of the whole of Romans as a pastoral conversation. To that end, here is one way (and not the only way) to capture the sweep of this inspiring letter. I draw here upon the work of Dr. William Greathouse in his book *Wholeness in Christ: Toward a Biblical Theology of Holiness*, specifically chapter 7.[5]

Romans 1–4

Paul is locating his holiness theology within the story of God with particular emphasis on how Jew and gentile both find themselves under the judgment of the law, but also that both have hope in the good news that we are justified by faith through the righteous faithfulness of Jesus Christ. "Abraham believed God, and it was reckoned to him as righteousness" (4:3, NRSV), a declaration that becomes paradigmatic for our faith in the resurrection of our Lord Jesus by which we can know forgiveness for sins and acceptance by a holy God. Paul says that what God declared over Abraham was not only for his sake but for ours. "It will be reckoned to us who believe in him who raised Jesus our Lord from the dead" (v. 24, NRSV). This lays the necessary foun-

---

5. William M. Greathouse, *Wholeness in Christ: Toward a Biblical Theology of Holiness* (Kansas City: Beacon Hill Press of Kansas City, 1998), 86–129.

dation for what it means to be reconciled to God in Christ and what it means to live the life of Christ in the world.

Romans 5

Having been justified by faith, we now enjoy "peace with God through our Lord Jesus Christ" (v. 1). This is the basis of our hope that Paul describes in the next verses, resulting not only in a way of looking toward our future but also in confidence for living in this world (including suffering) "because God's love has been poured out into our hearts through the Holy Spirit" (v. 5). The source of our confidence is God's love, which was and is demonstrated to us in God's willingness to gather into God's self in Christ all violence, abuse, and sin and deliver it to death on the cross; then through and over death by the power of resurrection. Therefore, we are reconciled to God, and we are "saved by his life" (v. 10, NRSV).

Paul then sets Adam and Christ side by side to connect the gospel of restoration, or holiness, to the whole story of God's relationship to humanity. Remembering the fall of Adam sets the backstory for the redemption that comes in Christ. Adam is a type, but Christ is the reality. As Dr. Greathouse says, "Adam is the shadow; Christ is the substance."[6] He goes on to explain that, "for Paul, Christ and Adam are . . . more than historical individuals; they are the heads of two contrasting yet overlapping orders of existence."[7]

"For as in Adam all die, so in Christ all will be made alive" (1 Cor. 15:22). Where sin brought death, now by grace, through faith, we can have "eternal life through Jesus Christ our Lord" (Rom. 5:21).

Part of the power of this text for holiness preaching is again to lay the necessary foundation for what God means to do for us "who once were far off" (Eph. 2:13, NRSV) but now can be brought into reconciled relationship with God because of God's love expressed and offered to us in Christ.

---

6. Ibid., 93.

7. Ibid., 94.

Romans 6

This chapter is one of the richest New Testament texts from which to preach and teach holiness as more than a second work of grace, within the gospel of sanctification holistically understood. Working from the foundation of justification by faith as response to God's grace, the question arises as to one's ongoing response to grace. Does it mean that one can now become careless and carefree in the conduct of one's life because grace will always deliver us from the burden of sin? "Shall we go on sinning so that grace may increase?" is the question Paul articulates in verse 1 on behalf of his audience. "*Me genioto!*" comes Paul's emphatic response, or, "May it never be!"

What is the basis of his objection? Paul goes on to say, in essence, *Do you not realize that there has been a death here? Nothing can ever be the same.* Through our baptism into Christ we are "buried with him by baptism into death" (v. 4, NRSV) so that we can also participate in new life through being raised with Christ. We can easily imagine our baptism and invite our hearers to reimagine theirs—when we were laid back into and under the water to image our being buried in death to the old life, and then we are joyfully lifted, raised up out of the water in ecstatic celebration of our new life! It is decisive and definitive, a moment of grace and faith in which something actually happens in the life of the believer and in the life of the congregation who welcomes the newly baptized into the household of faith. Christian baptism is and should be occasion to preach the good news of holiness, freedom from sin, and life in the power of the Spirit.

Paul's language is strong and decisive. We are "crucified" (v. 6) with Christ (echoes of Galatians 2:20) so that the "body of sin" ("our corporate existence in Adam")[8] "might be destroyed" (NRSV), "done away with" (NIV), or "lose its power" (NLT). This is good news that must be proclaimed to the people of God who so easily find them-

---

8. William M. Greathouse and George Lyons, *Romans 1-8: A Commentary in the Wesleyan Tradition, New Beacon Bible Commentary* (Kansas City: Beacon Hill Press of Kansas City, 2008), 182.

selves in a constant cycle of failure and forgiveness. Thank God for mercy and forgiveness, but the work of Christ means to accomplish more in us and in the world than forgiveness for sins committed. We are delivered, by the grace and power of God in Christ, from the "mastery" (v. 9) of sin. So we preach the good news: "consider yourselves dead to sin and alive to God in Christ Jesus" (v. 11, NRSV).

One might think, then, that having been delivered from sin's grip and united with Christ in his death, there is nothing more to be done. However, Paul turns immediately to exhort, "Therefore do not let sin reign" (v. 12). Wait a minute, I thought we were dead to sin, but now Paul warns about allowing sin to have continuing dominion over us? Which is it? The apostle is not suggesting that sin is no longer a possibility when we are united to Christ by faith and raised to new life. We now have the capacity in Christ to live differently than to be always under the tyranny of sin. Now we are able to do as Paul exhorts: "offer yourselves to God as those who have been brought from death to life" (v. 13). The reality of sanctifying faith is that we are free from sin (crisis) and are being freed from sin (process).

Dr. Randy Maddox writes that John Wesley's "clear concern was to preserve a dynamic tension that could celebrate whatever God's grace has already made possible in our lives, without relinquishing our responsibility to put that grace to work in the new areas that God continually brings to our attention."[9] Romans 6 is the dynamic daily reality of entire sanctification that celebrates the work of God to make us holy and anticipates the ongoing work of God to shape us more and more into the likeness of Christ. Here is where we can helpfully distinguish for our people that the language of "entire sanctification" does not mean the work of God in us is finished with nothing more to be done. The idea of "entire" here is about our whole-life offering to God, enabled by grace, nurtured by grace, and sustained by grace.

---

9. Randy L. Maddox, *Responsible Grace: John Wesley's Practical Theology* (Nashville: Kingswood Books, 1994), 190.

Romans 7

In chapter 7 the argument Paul is making may seem to take a detour, but he is simply focusing on those "brothers and sisters" (v. 1) who know the law—his Jewish people in Rome who have been formed to understand that holiness is a matter of adherence to Torah. However, gentiles also know something about the impulse to work toward achieving holiness through our efforts to obey God's law. Either way, Paul is reminding us that holiness of heart and life can never be reduced to a list of rules that we follow or even divine commands that we seek to satisfy through our obedience. Which is not to say, he hastens to affirm, that the law is sin. No, the law is an "expression of God's holiness."[10] God's law brings us to the awareness of our deep need for God's mercy and of the gracious work of Christ to do for and in us what the law of itself is unable to do.

This chapter is widely misunderstood and misapplied in Christian preaching. At first read, or in isolation from the fuller context, it may sound comforting. Perhaps Paul understands and affirms the struggle of Christian living, the ambiguity of religious life. Many read Romans 7 as salve for a troubled conscience when we experience disconnect between our testimony as followers of Jesus and our conduct in daily life. However, many scholars note that Paul is not reflecting on his present experience but "employing the historic present"[11] on his previous experience as a Pharisee. This is not endorsement of the commonly held notion of Christian life as ongoing struggle and regular failure but of the inability of adherence to the law to provide that for which the heart longs: freedom from sin. The law brings us to Christ in recognition of our complete dependency upon him to sanctify us and set us free from the dominion of sin. Thus, we get Paul's cry, "Who will rescue me from this body of death?" (v. 24, NRSV). Good news! There is an answer. "Thanks be to God through Jesus Christ our Lord!" (v. 25, NRSV).

---

10. Greathouse, *Wholeness in Christ*, 109.
11. Ibid., 110.

Romans 8

Now we are opened into another one of the richest of New Testament texts for the proclamation of the gospel of holiness. "Therefore" in verse 1 takes into view all that has been laid out beforehand and brings it to climactic expression: "There is now no condemnation for those who are in Christ Jesus, because through Christ Jesus the law of the Spirit who gives life has set you free from the law of sin and death" (vv. 1–2). We are invited into the embrace of life in the Spirit, which sets us free from life in the flesh (sarx). The flesh is delivered to death—for it is anti-Christ—but the body is transformed, enabling us to live the life of Jesus in this world and recognize God's redemptive work in all of creation.

In one of the most important texts of the Bible, Paul declares in this chapter God's project of setting all of creation free from its bondage to sin and death. And, as part of this redeeming, we live in the hope of "the redemption of our bodies" (v. 23) as we look forward to resurrection and the fulfillment of new creation. Living in this eschatological hope has everything to do with mindset (phronema), whereby we are formed into our right identity as children of God. There is a marked distinction between having a mind that is set on things of the flesh and a mind that is set on things of the Spirit (v. 5). A fleshly mindset is death, but a Spirit mindset is "life and peace" (v. 6). Within this rightly ordered mind, this rightly ordered life bearing, we also enjoy the graced confidence that we are beloved children who are able, through Christ, to turn from fear and run toward "Abba, Father" (v. 15), who, by the Spirit, bears witness to us that we are indeed the beloved of God.

The rich vein of resource that runs through this chapter is the simple yet profound line, "the Spirit of God lives in you" (v. 9). This is the great gift of the sanctified life: that God in Christ by the power and presence of the Spirit has taken up residence in us to cleanse, redeem, transform, sanctify, and send us (the people of God both individually and communally) back into the world as those now "conformed to the image of his Son" (v. 29). And this not for its own sake, nor for our benefit only, but that we might bear witness to the in-breaking reign of God in Christ Jesus. So together we sing:

"Called unto holiness," praise his dear name!

This blessed secret to faith now made plain:

Not our own righteousness, but Christ within,

Living, and reigning, and saving from sin.[12]

Romans 9–12

Having declared in the closing verses of chapter 8 that nothing can "separate us from the love of God that is in Christ Jesus our Lord" (v. 39), Paul turns in chapters 9 through 11 to a potential "congregational block"[13] that could be raised among his people. The truth is, God's people, Israel, find themselves cut off from the blessing that Paul has eloquently described. It breaks Paul's heart. Israel had every resource, every gift, and every possibility to live into the covenant established with Abraham. God is faithful to his promise, but the people have violated and broken the relationship time after time. In fact, in the midst of their disobedience and consequent suffering, Yahweh reveals long-suffering patience. So now the gentiles are invited into the provisions of God's covenant love—but not through their works of righteousness; it is by grace through faith, Paul repeats. He also wants his hearers to see and appreciate the patience of a God who remains faithful to the covenant in spite of Israel's disobedience.

We come to chapter 12 now, where the opening "therefore" once again places into our field of vision all that God is doing to redeem his people. There is a response that is called forth "in view of God's mercy" (v. 1). These verses—and, really, the remainder of the letter—challenge us to acknowledge and become accountable for the ways that God's gift of sanctifying grace should bear fruit in the life of individual believers and also the way believers live together in the

12. Leila N. Morris, "Holiness unto the Lord" in *Sing to the Lord* (Kansas City: Lillenas Publishing Company, 1993), no. 503.

13. The language of David Buttrick.

body of Christ and toward the world as a new creation community. These are powerful verses to call us to lives that are distinctive in the world. "Do not conform to the pattern of this world," Paul encourages, "but be transformed by the renewing of your mind" (v. 2). From this overarching rubric, the apostle lays out in practical fashion how the gospel of transformation works in the daily lives of God's people. A careful pastor, under the guidance and help of the Holy Spirit, can call forth over time and from these powerful texts a community of faith that begins to live together and toward the world as an authentic expression of the very kingdom of God.

For example, the exhortation to individuals that, if fully embraced, would create a new creation community is, "Do not think of yourself more highly than you ought" (v. 3). Paul goes on to describe in powerful language the shape of the sanctified community of faith. It is a place where the members celebrate their unity in the midst of amazing diversity. No one can be dismissed in terms of value to the whole. Here is a place where, following the clear pattern of Jesus, we lay down our lives in service to one another. This is the way of the sanctified life. Holiness of heart and life means nothing if it remains isolated and disconnected from others. Holiness is shaped, practiced, modeled, and embodied in the midst of communities of Christ followers who understand that "we are members one of another" (v. 5, NRSV). This may be one of the more sobering statements of the New Testament, for it is profoundly countercultural in terms of the ways the principalities and powers of this world tend to operate and assign value to things. The revival of the contemporary church could find its spring from the authentic, prayerful, and faithful practice of these words from Romans 12.

As we move further into the chapter, we begin to hear Paul's powerful descriptions of the marks of a sanctified people. They are practical yet can only find their practicability in the work of the Spirit through the surrendered lives of Christians. We hear of honoring one another above ourselves, of rejoicing in our hope in Christ while exercising patience in the inevitable sufferings that come with living in a fallen world. We hear of being concerned not only for our own lives but also focusing attention on one another so that, authentically, we can "weep with those who weep" and "rejoice with those who rejoice" (v. 15, NRSV). And finally, with echoes of our Lord's teaching in our ears, we are confronted with the truth that holiness people never take vengeance into their own hands but release judgment into the hands of God. This radical posture enables us to do the unthinkable, such as feed our enemies and give them something to drink (v. 20). If all of God's people, sanctified by the Spirit, were to live this way, it would transform the world.

Romans 13–16

These chapters continue to outline how this great grace is lived throughout our relationships in the church and in the world. What does a sanctified life look like in relationship to governing authorities? How does it look with our most proximate neighbors? What does it demand when we find ourselves in disagreements with one another, particularly over the practices and behaviors of how a Christian life should rightly be conducted in the world? These chapters press the truth that there is nothing in our total experience that is outside of God's concern and nothing beyond the influence of a life lived in total devotion to God. As Paul Achtemeier writes, "God's lordship, which in Christ has begun to be re-established over his rebellious creation, is not limited to certain areas of human life which have to do with 'religion.' That lordship is exercised over the whole of creation; and nothing in that creation, religious or secular, is beyond the power and purposes of God."[14]

Although my brief summary cannot do it justice, I trust we can begin to see something of the powerful and rich resource of Romans for holiness preaching. Pastors would do well to study these texts prayerfully and carefully. These are the scriptures to which we are

---

14. Paul Achtemeier, Romans, Interpretation: A Bible Commentary for Teaching and Preaching (Louisville, KY: John Knox Press, 1985), 206.

sent by the Spirit in service to God's people. We are sent to shepherd, love, and proclaim to them the good news of God's sanctifying grace. Our primary motivation for preaching from these powerful texts can never be to impress or entertain. It must always be a motivation born of love; that our people would know God, love God, and serve God with all of their hearts, minds, souls, and strength.

Clearly, there are many other wonderful textual resources for preaching holiness, as we briefly reviewed in the previous chapter. It is my hope that walking with you through these key scriptures will spark your own imagination and hunger to work at preaching a gospel that is never reduced to "three steps to success" or "how to have a happy life" but that truly proclaims the good news of holiness of heart and life, made possible by the love of God in Christ, who—through his birth, life, death, resurrection, and ascension—offers to us not only forgiveness of sins but freedom from sin. Pastor, I plead with you to be faithful to this work. Holiness of heart and life is the hope-filled message that we were raised up to preach. Let us seek it, pray for it, learn it, live it, and proclaim it to the glory of God and the edification of the church.

5 THE HOLINESS OF THE CHURCH*

I trust that by this point in the book, it is clear that holiness of heart and life is conceived not only as a personal and individual experience but is also inexorably linked with the life of the community of faith. John Wesley's proclamation is well known among us: "There is no holiness but social holiness." The larger context of Wesley's axiom is instructive: "Solitary religion is not to be found there. 'Holy Solitaries' is a phrase no more consistent with the gospel than 'Holy Adulterers.' The gospel of Christ knows of no religion but social; no holiness but social holiness. Faith, working by love, is the length and breadth and depth and height of Christian perfection."[1]

The congregation that raised me in the faith taught me that the supreme concern of Christian faith was my personal relationship with Jesus Christ. I am profoundly thankful that they taught me about God's love for me personally and that God welcomes me—through justification, regeneration, and adoption—into intimate relationship with the Father, Son, and Holy Spirit. They also taught me that my relation-

---

1. John Wesley, "List of Poetical Works," *Works of John Wesley*, 3rd ed., *Vol. XIV* (Kansas City: Beacon Hill Press of Kansas City, 1978), 14:321.

---

*Based on a paper by the author, presented at the Global Theology Conference of the Church of the Nazarene, Guatemala City, Guatemala, April 2002.

ship to God must be intentionally nurtured through the disciplines of spiritual formation, and I am thankful for that as well. However, I was not greatly challenged to understand life in Christ as *life together*. We certainly enjoyed the fellowship of brothers and sisters in the congregation, and we knew the importance of cooperation to accomplish the work of ministry, but there was no real sense of being formed *as a people* in the way of Jesus and for the world. This would have been only in the sense of the sum of each one's spiritual health. While it is certainly true that each member's spiritual vitality has an influence on the whole, the awareness of my vital connection to the body of Christ, including an attitude and posture of submission to the authority of the church, was not highly developed in our congregation.

I have discovered across these many years of ministry that the way I learned was shared by many. It is clear to me that the majority of persons in our churches still think of discipleship as mostly a personal, and even a private, matter. This mindset has been systematically and skillfully encouraged by an American society that is committed to individuality and personal freedom. We are shaped every day to think in terms of what is best for us, what we prefer, and how some ideal of a good life is found in consumption and acquisition. American life forms us in the values and priorities of capitalism. James K. A. Smith currently articulates this as well as anyone in his work around the idea of "cultural liturgies" that form us in these ways.[2] These cultural liturgies exert a profound influence on the church in our time and location. In the midst of this milieu, holiness preaching has too often been presented as an individual and even private transaction and usually in terms of personal piety, which is an important but narrow understanding of holiness.

---

2. See Smith's three-volume *Cultural Liturgies* series (Grand Rapids: Baker Academic): *Desiring the Kingdom* (2009), *Imagining the Kingdom* (2013), and *Awaiting the King* (2017); see also *You Are What You Love: The Spiritual Power of Habit* (Grand Rapids: Brazos Press, 2016).

There are several artifacts to point to this reality. For example, there is a common lack of intimacy among God's people that reflects not only a cultural belief in the sovereignty of the individual but also the assumption that we generally ought not to be getting involved in the holiness of others. No wonder our people so easily move from one congregation to another on little other basis than some vague notion that their personal needs are not being met. There is a kind of "bootstraps theology" at work, whereby people believe that being reconciled to God is mostly their own responsibility. A general lack of self-disclosure and accountability has made the idea of church discipline repulsive and the practice virtually nonexistent.

Although the Bible clearly calls us to "submit to one another out of reverence for Christ" (Eph. 5:21), this largely remains an unrealized ideal or vague notion of being kind to one another. We could sure use more kindness in the church, but the apostle's idea of submitting to one another has to do with speaking truth to each other, correcting each other, calling one another to account for the conduct of our lives, and the actionable commitment to lay down our lives for one another. We are familiar with Wesley's strategy for this, which was gathering Christians into small groups on a weekly basis where they called each other to account for the practices of Christlike living. A church that is committed to holiness of heart and life will be committed to far more than proclaiming a doctrine and calling people to a visible response (such as prayer at the altar)—as helpful as these may be. Holiness people are committed to getting involved in one another's holiness, to telling the truth about ourselves, and to helping each other turn from the values and priorities of this world and run toward the values and priorities of the kingdom of God.

Please do not misunderstand me on this point. The grace of entire sanctification is thoroughly personal. A life marked by the very character and spirit of Jesus is personal, but it is not private. The New Testament vision of holiness finds its full meaning only as sanctified persons see themselves essentially as part of a sanctified church. Jesus's prayer for us is a corporate prayer: "Sanctify them by the truth" (John

17:17). Everywhere the New Testament places the idea of a sanctified discipleship squarely within the context of the community of faith. Even as Jesus continues his prayer he says, "May they . . . be one as we are one" (vv. 21–22). Jesus expects that the perfect community of the Godhead will be reflected in the community of saints. The letters of Paul to the churches are replete with exhortations toward holiness, calling the people to live together under the lordship of Jesus Christ and in the power of the Holy Spirit.[3] The point of these observations for our present considerations is that our expressions of holiness doctrine and our preaching of holiness must bear witness to the fact that the *whole* people of God are called to be holy by command and by provision. The Scriptures seem to have in mind more than a simple collection of holy *ones*.

We confess together when we recite the Apostles' Creed that we believe in "the holy catholic church." But in what sense is the church holy? Most of us are keenly aware of what H. Ray Dunning calls "the obvious unholiness of the empirical church."[4] Much of daily pastoral work rises from the failure of the community of faith to reflect the character of "a holy nation" (1 Pet. 2:9). Nevertheless, we are persuaded that God is calling not only individuals to be holy but also the church. The question is, *In what ways is biblical holiness corporate and not individual only?* I offer four observations on how local congregations can grow in the understanding, experience, and practice of corporate holiness in addition to the necessary proclamation of this understanding from pulpits.

First, the worship of local congregations must be firmly rooted in the historic Christian faith. Too many pastors order worship around pragmatic concerns, or to put it plainly, in what will gather a crowd. I agree with Professor Marva Dawn when she says that "so many de-

---

3. Rom. 13:8–10; 15:5–7; 1 Cor. 1:2; 12:12–13; Gal. 5:16–26; Eph. 1:1–14; 2:19–22; 4:1–5:20; Col. 3:12–17.

4. H. Ray Dunning, *Grace, Faith, and Holiness: A Wesleyan Systematic Theology* (Kansas City: Beacon Hill Press of Kansas City, 1988), 532.

cisions are being based on criteria other than the most essential—namely, that God be the Subject and Object . . . of our worship."[5] Holiness is nothing if not the change of life focus from self to God. The acts of the worshiping community are essential to this understanding and experience. For example, we need worship that places high priority on the Eucharist, that we might regularly (yes, even weekly, which is the practice of the historic Christian church) receive grace to live together as kingdom people. We need worship that is organized around something deeper than self-serving national holidays but, rather, around the story of redemption. We need to recover the appropriateness and importance of corporate confession. How would the church be changed through weekly praying together the Collect for Purity or other prayers of confession? The corporate prayer of confession in the worship of the community of faith would make most sense when the congregation is invited to the Lord's Table each week. Here is where we are remembered as the body of Christ, formed as the people of God, and given the gift of an identity and purpose that is rooted in the gospel of Jesus Christ.

Second, preaching the holiness of the church will require a focus on Christian forgiveness. Of course, the larger issue is love, which is central to the whole idea of holiness, but I put it this way because what most damages authentic corporate holiness is unforgiveness. Christian relationships afford us ample opportunity for real experiences of self-sacrificing love, the essence of holiness. In John's account of the Pentecost event, the risen Jesus says to his disciples after breathing on them, "Receive the Holy Spirit" (20:22). Then he immediately (textually) speaks of the necessity of forgiveness between them. Forgiveness lies at the very heart of the gospel and of Christian holiness. Where holiness is rightly and regularly preached, it would be untenable for our people to testify to holiness of heart and life and remain in broken relationships with one another. As this happens, and it is far too

---

5. Marva J. Dawn, *A Royal "Waste" of Time: The Splendor of Worshiping God and Being Church for the World* (Grand Rapids: William B. Eerdmans Publishing Company, 1999), 8.

regular, our witness is compromised, and our power for service in the name of Jesus is diminished. I submit that what weakens too many of our churches is the reality of unforgiveness between people of the congregation. Holiness preaching should and can call this to account and proclaim hope that our risen Lord knows how to bring renewal and life where we would only expect brokenness and death.

The third critical component for corporate holiness is unity. Christian unity is the indisputable sign that the people of God have surrendered their own interests to the kingdom interest of serving God and neighbor. This kind of unity is an important part of holiness, not only within congregations but also in terms of the unity that crosses institutional, national, economic, racial, and gender barriers. Where holiness is active the typical prejudices, discriminations, and suspicions between people are disempowered. I suspect that most of our people would say yes and amen to these affirmations, but in order for these commitments to have credibility, they must become actionable in particular ways within the community of faith. With the growing ethnic diversity of American communities, the church of Jesus has before it a critical opportunity to demonstrate in our gathered congregations the inclusive and richly diverse nature of the kingdom of God. This requires the intentional work of leadership to challenge our people beyond the comfort of homogeneity and into the truly missionary movements of Christian life, which—following the initiating movement of God toward us—crosses any boundary to extend love to the outsider, marginalized, and prejudicially dismissed. Faithful holiness preaching must include calls to unity.

The fourth element is service. Corporate holiness is much more than a group of Christians being pious. It is the community of faith actively serving each other and engaging a broken world with acts of sacrificial love and service as depicted in Acts 2:42 or as Jesus illustrated in Matthew 25, to name only two examples among many. Our historic connection of holiness and compassion is not only a beautiful and compelling part of our heritage, it also bears the seeds of our continuing future as emerging generations seek faith expressions that understand a pious life as much more than adherence to a list of behavioral preferences, no matter how legitimate they may be. Holiness, in order to be scriptural, must always have in its heart the way our Lord understood and proclaimed the signs of God's reign: "The Spirit of the Lord is on me, because he has anointed me to proclaim good news to the poor. He has sent me to proclaim freedom for the prisoners and recovery of sight for the blind, to set the oppressed free, to proclaim the year of the Lord's favor" (Luke 4:18–19).

The holiness of the church is vitally connected to the holiness of persons. Holiness preachers would do well to study the helpful work by Dr. Thomas Noble *Holy Trinity, Holy People: The Theology of Christian Perfecting*. Noble beautifully frames the doctrine of entire sanctification within a communal and Trinitarian understanding of the people of God as the location for what he helpfully terms "Christian perfecting." Laying out in challenging but accessible fashion theological affirmations on the Persons of the Godhead, Dr. Noble writes, "One cannot separate their being from their interpersonal relations. They do not first exist and *then* relate to each other. They exist (or better 'subsist') in their relationship to each other."[6] It is the beautiful idea of *perichoresis*, or "mutual in-dwelling" as the "indivisible" God. "God is three *Persons*, but not three individuals."[7] From this foundation we begin to understand more deeply the idea of a holy church. "Only then within the church—which is the fellowship (*koinonia*) of the Father and the Son in the Holy Spirit and within which the Spirit includes us by uniting us to Christ—can we articulate what the holiness of God is."[8] And thus, "The church corporately (rather than merely the individual Christian) is the image of God that reflects God's holiness."[9] This deep understanding of the life of the church reflecting the holiness of God

6. Noble, *Holy Trinity: Holy People*, 218.
7. Ibid.
8. Ibid., 219.
9. Ibid.

is a much-needed understanding from which contemporary holiness preaching needs to find its foundation and its most compelling vision.

PART THREE

HOW Should Holiness Be Preached?

6 HOMILETICAL CONSIDERATIONS

While homiletical considerations are not unique to holiness preaching, any work on preaching should help us think about the practice of preaching. How we *say* the sermon is part of the content. Although the Holy Spirit inspires and uses all kinds of voices and styles for the proclamation of the gospel, these matters are not incidental to the task of good preaching. The way we voice a sermon (thinking of both writing and aurality) is not only about capturing the interest of hearers but is also involved with the work of the Spirit in landing the truth of the text into receptive hearts in a way that draws out the response of the hearers. This response is not and must never be essentially response to the preacher's artful or entertaining delivery or charismatic personality but always response to the present work of the Spirit in the gathered body of Christ to guide, correct, convict, and enable the personal and corporate amen to the gospel. This does not suggest that the manner of delivery is a minor note in the labor of gospel proclamation. Imaginative speech (to borrow Walter Brueggemann's language) is so important to effective hearing of the gospel that its intentional development is a holy obligation of one who would preach.

Preaching is an art. Therefore, the task of preaching well can never be reduced to certain can't-miss structures or formulae that will always enable the sermon to work. However, it can be argued that preaching is also science, in a way, in that there are certain skills, tools, and understandings of form that enable the crafting and delivery of a faithful sermon. Part of learning to preach well is being unafraid to consider oneself novice, always in need of learning, growing, and working to find our unique voice as a servant of the Word. Because of the artful nature of preaching, one can gain some sense of mastery in the work—but never in the sense of knowing all there is to know about the task.

Good preachers are always digging deeper into the body of learning, literature, and practice of homiletics. Gladly, we are flush with resources in this regard, having access to the helpful works of people like David Buttrick, Fred Craddock, Eugene Lowry, Anna Carter Florence, Thomas Long, Barbara Brown Taylor, Craig Barnes, Luke Powery, and many others. And, closer in, we have numerous colleagues within our own movement from whom we can learn and with whom we can grow in our preaching. Part of the journey of learning to preach well is to gather good resources to help us not only with the work of exegeting texts but also with forming and delivering the sermon. Every growing preacher I know is a person who reads those who teach preachers, listens to the preaching of effective pastors, and never settles into the type of arrogant, got-it-all-figured-out mindset that stunts our growth and could cause us to become stagnant.

There are a number of considerations as we think about homiletics. We need to think about context and culture, in that sermons are located in particular places and in the midst of particular people with stories and experiences that will shape how they hear the sermon. We need to think about language, narrative, and story from the recognition that we are a storied people, especially as people who locate our identity within the story of God. Although we live in a digital age and information technology is ubiquitous, we navigate our way in the world through narration. Whether interpersonal relationships or world news, the narrative nature of societies forms how we learn about the world, how we know ourselves in relation to others, and how we make all manner of decisions about the daily conduct of our lives. We need to think about structure and form as these become part of the sermon content, either to enhance the saying and hearing of the message or possibly to hinder and block effective communication. We also need to think about the sound of the sermon. This may be included under form, but I find it to be so critical to effective preaching that I think it warrants some focused discussion. So let's work with these in turn and consider possible gaps in our own development where we can focus on growing in our homiletical skill.

Context and Culture

Context and culture are the work of congregational exegesis. Sermons never develop in isolation but, at their best, articulate the hope of the gospel in ways that connect to the culture and context of particular congregations. I prefer to think of the pastor or preacher as one who is drawn out by the Spirit from the congregation then equipped, trained, ordained, and sent back to the congregation as embodiment of the Good Shepherd who knows the sheep and whom the sheep know and whose voice they trust. I know I am tipping my bias toward parish ministry here, but I do know something about the difference between pastoral preaching and itinerant preaching. Having spent twenty-five years in pastoral preaching followed by twelve years in itinerant preaching, there is a marked and substantive difference in these ministry assignments. Itinerant preaching certainly has its necessary and helpful place, but there is a tremendous advantage when one has intimate knowledge of the people to whom one is preaching and about the cultural location in which the sermon will be given.

In this way, congregations are partners in the proclamation of the gospel. As a pastor, I knew that some of my people made it their practice to pray for me throughout the week. Several of these routinely gathered around me on Sunday mornings prior to the service to pray the Spirit's anointing over me and over the service. When we have the privilege of knowing a congregation well, we also enjoy the benefit of having them in the study with us, so to speak. There is a sense of the congregation looking over our shoulder as we prepare, and the thoughtful preacher is always aware of this connection, seeing in one's mind and heart the stories of the beloved who will gather on Sunday for worship. The way this works best is when the preacher or pastor is deeply engaged in the lives of the people. Pastoral visitation and conversations are an essential part of the work of good preaching because this is part of what helps answer the "so what?" question in everything a preacher will say. Fred Craddock suggested that during preparation the preacher literally write the words, "So what?" at the top of the page and keep that question in mind as every decision is made about what to say and what not to say.

This contextual awareness is essential for good holiness preaching because the preacher needs a keen focus on what is happening in the lives of the congregation. Where do they most find it a struggle to live a Christlike life? What questions or objections would they raise to some of the biblical affirmations or exhortations toward a holy life? The preacher's knowledge of these things matures over time as the story of pastor and people develops across a multitude of shared experiences. This is why I believe there is great value in sustained pastoral tenure. It is not only about one's knowledge of the location and people, but it also has something to do with being accepted by the indigenous people as someone who knows them, understands where they live, and cares for them.

Part of this understanding of culture and context is about recognizing the capacity that the congregation may or may not have for hearing and receiving particular points of content. The preacher needs to understand the kind of education these people have received. What sort of local preferences do they embrace in terms of music, food, play, work, rest, etc.? Will these folks understand and appreciate the cultural references I may offer in the sermon? I love baseball and love to tell stories about baseball that I think have great connection to life in general, but not everyone can understand and appreciate these references, so I have to be careful. In this regard, the preacher's own life is part of the content of preaching. We bear witness to the gospel from the unique story of our own lives, yet we must exercise care that our testimony does not become a congregational block.

Thinking about these things, it is no wonder that the act of preaching is such a vulnerable act in many ways. We are not only explaining the text, but we are also laying bare our own engagement with the text—the ways in which the Spirit has spoken to us and begun to rearrange our lives in response to the Word. I have heard a number of fellow ministers describe a common dream preachers have, the vision of standing to preach without being fully clothed, and no wonder! This is no simple task of entertaining a crowd; this is loving a people by doing the difficult work of listening deeply to what the Spirit would say to the church and then finding a way to gain a hearing for that word among a people who may or may not be ready to hear. Hard work, indeed!

Language, Narrative, and Story

Before we get to how we will voice the sermon, we have to work hard at deciding on the words we will use. Words are important, even though contemporary culture throws around words like so much chaff. Good preachers do not wait for the inspiration of the moment to decide how best to articulate the truth that has emerged from the careful study of Scripture. The best preachers work intentionally on syntax, grammar, and vocabulary. This is certainly not to suggest a cold reading of the sermon from a manuscript. Many preachers who write carefully do so in order to catalogue in their minds the kinds of words and phrases to which they will reach in the preaching of the message without a manuscript. Notes or no notes is not the question here, in itself. This is about recognizing the power of language and the compelling nature of narrative and story so that the heart of the message has a chance to find a hearing.

Another sense in which we need to appreciate story is the absolute necessity for faithful Christian preaching to rise from the Bible. It may seem that this should go without saying, but I have not always found this to be the case. On far too many occasions, it was evident to me that a preacher decided what they wanted to say before they ever went to the text, and then the use of the Bible was only to find some verses in support of what they had already decided to say. Holiness preaching can easily fall into this trap if we approach it primarily from a doctrinal or apologetic framework, as discussed earlier. Here is where there is great wisdom in the long-standing practice of the church to assign certain biblical texts for each Sunday of the Christian year.

I recognize that many preachers in our tradition have not been Lectionary preachers, and I am not arguing for use of the Lectionary for its own sake. However, the theological intention with which these texts are gathered and organized is a valuable tool for pastors and congregations who recognize that we live under a wisdom that is larger than our own experience. A temptation for most of us would be to default to texts with which we are most familiar, which is dangerous because we have a tendency to stop hearing familiar texts. The discipline of preaching from assigned texts does several things. It presses us to grow in our work of study and learning. It reminds us that there is something larger going on each Sunday than whatever is happening in my one location. And it nudges us toward one another, as we help each other and learn from one another in wrestling with the readings for each Sunday. Wonderful resources are emerging that not only give the preacher content but also spark encouragement as we collectively listen to the Spirit who is at work to speak to God's people through the "foolishness of preaching" (see 1 Cor. 1:21).

This kind of servant mindset reminds us that the work of a preacher is not for its own sake and certainly not for the edification of the preacher alone. The best way to understand this is the way Thomas Long puts it when he suggests that the preacher goes to the text in service to the congregation. "So, the preacher goes to the scripture, but not alone. The preacher goes on behalf of the faithful community and, in a sense, on behalf of the world."[1] Then, when Scripture, by the power of the Spirit, has done its work on the preacher, the preacher is able to come to the congregation and joyfully announce, "Thus says

---

1. Thomas G. Long, *The Witness of Preaching* (Louisville, KY: Westminster John Knox Press, 1989), 45.

the Lord." In this sense, as a number of women preachers have helped us to see, sermons are not simply crafted; they are birthed. We are not in control; we are servants of the Word. I will confess that there have been times when I thought I *was* in control. Sometimes I brought a sermon to the people about which I thought, *This is really good.* And it fell flat. Other times—well, you know how this goes. The point is, we are not working alone. Thanks be to God!

In my work as a district superintendent, going from church to church, I discovered a widespread hunger among God's people for authentic biblical preaching. In many contexts, people have grown weary of preaching that only touches the surface. Topical preaching may have its place, but even then it must be done by the pastor taking a contemporary problem or issue to the Bible in search of God's answer—not in a proof-texting way but in a way that finds its basis in love and not laziness. People know when the preacher has not personally and deeply engaged the text. And this has to do not only with content but also with the manner in which the sermon is voiced. Imaginative preaching in terms of language takes work; it requires time and intention to craft the kind of speaking that engages people and elicits what Craddock called the "nod of recognition."[2]

Preaching that attends to language, narrative, and story is able to locate any particular text within the grand sweep of the story of God. How does this episode, this song, this poem, this sermon, or this letter fit in to the overall story that is the Bible, which means to invite us into participation in the mission of God to redeem all things? One Church of the Nazarene preacher I listen to often is Dr. Scott Daniels. What Pastor Scott models so well in his preaching is not only his substantive understanding of the text—and not only great pastoral care in terms of congregational exegesis—but also his ability to locate every text and every sermon within the sweeping story of God's redemption. Scott acknowledges that he can hardly preach any sermon without saying something about Exodus, which is not simply his personal

---

2. Fred B. Craddock, *Preaching* (Nashville: Abingdon Press, 1985), 160.

preference for a particular book or genre; rather, it is about the way the story of the redemption of God's people, Israel, is paradigmatic and instructive for what God continues to do in and for God's people called the church.

A key tool for constructing sermons that are faithful to the text is always to ask the question of how this text functioned for its first hearers and, thus, how it would intend to re-function now. Craddock asks it this way: "Does the sermon do and say what the biblical text does and says?"[3] For example, if one preaches from the prophet Amos and the people go away from the service feeling giddy and happy, the text likely did not re-function faithfully. Conversely, if one preaches from 1 Peter and the people are depressed, the text likely did not re-function faithfully. Obviously, applications are updated as we take contemporary lives to the text, but the heart or truth of the text will re-function across multiple contexts.

Structure and Form

These thoughts raise the issue of structure and form, which is actually a fairly challenging point of consideration when it comes to faithful preaching. As Tom Long says, "Sermon form is a curious beast."[4] Part of the challenge is that we are not simply talking about something we write down on paper. Preaching is a performative event that happens in the convergence between the prepared, Spirit-anointed preacher and the prayerfully prepared, anticipating congregation. When all are giving themselves to these things faithfully, amazing moments of God's presence are realized.

We cannot think that sermon structure and form are a simple matter of making a cool decision about the framework on which the proclamation of a particular text will best be carried. Long says, "In the simplest of terms, a sermon form is an organizational plan for deciding what kinds of things will be said and done in a sermon and

---

3. Ibid., 28.
4. Long, *The Witness of Preaching*, 92.

in what sequence."[5] What Long says is true, but there is also an intuitive feature to this work, particularly for the pastoral preacher who is discerning all the components that go into the preaching moment in a certain time and place. My reason for noting this is to suggest that there is no right answer when it comes to sermon structure and form. A particular text could conceivably be preached well from a number of forms because the context of the sermon will always be unique. Again, the question to discern is about what kind of form will allow the text to re-function faithfully in the hearing of this people, in this location, and at this time, and what sermon form will allow the text to function according to its genre.

Most preachers who have studied homiletics have their preferred structures. Fred Craddock argued strongly for the inductive form, taking the congregation with you through discovery of the text and toward a shared *aha!* moment and response. We can think about plots, pages, loops, and other ways of structuring the sequencing of logic and movements, but each of these carries a basic structure that can be described as Need, Answer, and Response.[6] This is all predicated upon listening to and engaging the text, which is about exegesis and prayerful discernment. But then we can begin to structure the sermon around these three questions:[7]

1. What is the *need* of the passage? This refers to the basic human problem or question that a passage of Scripture is addressing. These human needs can be explicit in the words of the text or implicit through the theme or mood of the text. Need can be as general as the problem of sin, or as specific as how a Christian deals with the loss of

---

5. Ibid., 93.

6. The descriptions here appeared in the Advent 2000 issue of *Preacher's Magazine*, which was co-edited by the present author and David Busic.

7. Henry Mitchell suggests a fourfold pattern: situation, complication, resolution, celebration. Henry H. Mitchell, *Celebration and Experience in Preaching* (Nashville: Abingdon Press, 1990).

a loved one. The task of the preacher is to locate the problem in the text so that resolution can begin to take place through the sermon.[8]

2. What is *God's answer* to that need? Just as every passage deals with a basic human dilemma, so every passage also offers God's answer to that problem. Any sermonic attempts to provide answers to human problems outside of the grace of God is only a disguised form of legalism, or trying to do for ourselves what only God can do for us. Until the preacher can give God's answer to the problem, the sermon is not ready to be preached. A helpful way to identify what God is going to do about a human problem is to discern the image of God being portrayed in the passage. Simply offering solutions that cause people to work harder or do more is to deny the power of God to change a heart.

3. How does the passage call us to *respond*? While hope for human need rests in God's grace and not our endeavors, good preaching insists that people respond to God's activity in their lives. The faithful proclamation of God's Word always calls forth a decision. The response can be manifested outwardly, through an altar call or invitational movement toward the Lord's Table. The response can also be an inward call to repentance, gratitude, consecration, endurance, confession, hope for the future, or obedience. Often the response will naturally flow out of the function of the form (genre) of the passage.

A passage of Scripture can be *explained* without answering these questions of theological reflection, but it cannot be *proclaimed* until we understand the human problem, God's answer, and our response to God's grace.

A couple of special notes around form may be helpful. First, to use an aeronautics analogy, I have witnessed many struggle to take off and struggle to land. Once we have the core content and key moves of the sermon, we need to think carefully about how to invite the congregation into the hearing of the sermon. The preacher has a few seconds

---

8. I am mindful of my earlier call for preaching to keep Genesis 1 and 2 in mind as God's good creation sets the place from which to start in terms of knowing there is a problem.

in the opening of a sermon (probably not more than two minutes) to answer the hearers' implicit question, *Why should I get involved with this?* It's the ultimate "so what?" criterion. All good narrative forms draw in the auditor with a question, dilemma, or recognition that interests them and sparks a desire to hear what the Bible might have to say about this issue. On the other side, the work of crafting a good sermon is about knowing what not to say and knowing where to stop. I have heard lots of preachers deliver two or three sermons for the price of one. This is not usually because the content demands it but due to a lack of skillful structure or focus that can be disciplined enough to leave lots of content unused.

One other note has to do with the use of images. The use of something like PowerPoint, photos, or videos can certainly enhance the proclamation when used skillfully. The problem is that few preachers actually have the skill to pull this off; thus, these become a distraction or utterly beside the point. Unless you have access to professional skill in these areas, I urge a judicious use of these tools (less is more).

Sound

Preaching is both oral (spoken) and aural (heard). Therefore, good preaching attends to what I call the *music* of preaching. By this I mean that the way we speak the sermon in the context of a congregation must pay attention to things like tone, rhythm, pitch, tempo, and dynamic. Dan Boone writes that "the first preparatory act of preaching is to attend to the Word through the ears."[9] He is talking about taking in a text through all of the senses, but especially hearing, since that is how these texts were accessed and delivered for centuries prior to the printed page being available to all. Plus, many of them were initially gathered through narrative or oral tradition—the telling and repeating of these stories from place to place and generation to generation. Therefore, how a sermon sounds is a significant part of how

---

9. Dan Boone, *Preaching the Story That Shapes Us* (Kansas City: Beacon Hill Press of Kansas City, 2008), 75.

it is received. I recommend, especially early in one's ministry, that preachers regularly listen to recordings or, even better, watch videos of their preaching. It is not easy at first, but the discipline can help us to hear and see things (like movements) in our delivery that clearly need adjustment or improvement. Also, if we have the courage, we should invite others with skill in judging these things to tell us the truth about whether our articulation of the message is coming across.

John Wesley was concerned with how his preachers would say the sermon. He understood that the wrong style could hinder the proclamation of the gospel. He gives "Directions Concerning Pronunciation and Gesture," which consists of several pages of practical advice and direction, majoring on managing the sound of one's voice and the movements of one's body. Among the advices are what he calls the "chief faults of speaking," as listed here:

1. The speaking too loud. This is disagreeable to the hearers, as well as inconvenient for the speaker.

2. The speaking too low. This is, of the two, more disagreeable than the former. Take care, therefore, to keep between the extremes; to preserve the key, the command of your voice.

3. The speaking in a thick cluttering manner. Some persons mumble, or swallow some words or syllables, and do not utter the rest articulately or distinctly.

4. The speaking too fast. This is a common fault; but not a little one; particularly when we speak of the things of God.

5. The speaking too slow is not a common fault; and when we are once warned of it, it may be easily avoided.

6. The speaking with an irregular, desultory and uneven voice, raised or depressed unnaturally or unseasonably.

7. But the greatest and most common fault of all is, the speaking with a tone: some have a . . . squeaking tone; some a singing or canting one; some an high, swelling theatrical tone, laying too much emphasis on every sentence; some have an awful, solemn tone; others an odd, whimsical, whining tone, not to be expressed in words.[10]

---

10. Wesley, "Directions Concerning Pronunciation and Gesture," *Works*, 13:518.

These notes could be dismissed as archaic with no correspondence to our time, but I encourage us to consider what Wesley is trying to do here. He clearly understands that how we say the sermon is an essential part of proclamation and cannot be ignored. Working to improve the sound of our preaching has nothing to do with being considered a good or pleasant preacher for its own sake. It has everything to do with making sure the preacher does not become a block or barrier to what the Spirit through the text wants to say to the church.

Allow me now to ask you to reflect on your work of preaching. Are you guarding sufficient spaces in your weekly rhythm to sit prayerfully with the text and listen for the unmistakable promptings of the Spirit? Are you resisting the temptation to rush too soon to other helpers? Nothing can replace the preacher's own engagement with the reading and study of Scripture. Wesley practiced and taught that one should never sit down to read the Bible without first praying for the gift of illumination by the power of the Spirit who is our guide. Are you listening well to your people? The best preaching rises from pastoral love that is grounded in everyday, real-life engagement with people who are walking the way of Jesus, or perhaps walking away from Jesus. May the Lord help you, Pastor, to remember the first two "core duties" given to us in the Manual for the Church of the Nazarene: "to pray" and "to preach the Word."[11] May your preaching flow from God's love "poured into our hearts through the Holy Spirit that has been given to us" (Rom. 5:5, NRSV).

When we focus on homiletics, as we must do, it can be tempting to think that good preaching depends on our skill and our efforts. Both are involved and must be attended to. However, we must never forget that we are utterly dependent on the work of the Holy Spirit in the task of preaching. As a pastor, my penultimate act of preparation was to go to the sanctuary early on Sunday morning and preach

---

11. *Church of the Nazarene Manual: 2017–2021* (Kansas City: Nazarene Publishing House, 2017), 200.

my sermon aloud to the empty space. I needed to hear it in the room and feel myself say it. I wanted to get the rhythm of it—the music of it—centered in my body. Once this was done, the most important preparation of all happened as I cast myself across the altar of the church and cried out to God for the help that only God could provide. And in twenty-five years of pastoral preaching, I discovered that God is faithful. Thanks be to God!

7 LIFE TOGETHER: HOLY MISSION

Holiness preaching that finds its way into the heart and practice of God's people cannot be dislocated from the holistic life of the congregation. As previously noted, holiness has too often been understood in terms of individuals rather than communities. We discussed the nature of a holy church in chapter 5, but what about the ways in which a holy church participates in God's redemptive mission in the world? There is much good thinking, writing, and preaching around this question, but a book on preaching holiness cannot ignore what the gospel of holiness of heart and life means for how the people of God are to embody the sanctified life together.

There are many possible approaches to this large question. I find significant pastoral guidance in the epistle of 1 Peter. The location of this epistle seems increasingly familiar to us. First Peter is *paranesis*, which means in part that its primary function is to exhort, admonish, strengthen, and encourage a church living in troubled times. It is written to God's "chosen" ones, God's "sanctified" ones (1:2, NRSV), yet they find themselves as strangers in the world, bearing witness to a faith that is under suspicion. For the recipients of this letter, bearing the name "Christian" could make life difficult, if not dangerous.

Peter's audience is often described as a church under persecution. Some scholars argue it was not primarily persecution in the sense of martyrdom, although that certainly did happen. It is more often like discrimination because these Christians would not participate in many of the cultural practices of their pagan neighbors. Lately, we have been using the language of "exile" and "dislocation," reflecting on how our experience of being Christians, or at least of being church people, is changing in the twenty-first century. So we may think we have something in common with Peter's audience, and in one way we do, but I have some questions about that. Is it true that our lives are so distinctive in this world that it causes folks to do a double take and wonder what makes us as we are? Or do we mostly fit in, blend in, and go along with society? Is it true that we are so much like Jesus that our way of life stands out and draws our neighbors to want to know why we live as we do?

Peter's challenge to these early Christians is to "live such good lives among the pagans that, though they accuse you of doing wrong, they may see your good deeds and glorify God on the day he visits us" (2:12). Peter says throughout the letter that much of living these good lives has to do with how we treat each other in the body of Christ and also with the way we respond when we suffer discrimination for following Jesus. We do not respond to discrimination and threats with our own discrimination and threats. We do not respond to a changing world by grasping for the same tools that our world reaches for to try and secure our own lives. We "sanctify Christ as Lord" (3:15, NRSV).

This is why 1 Peter resonates with what holiness might mean, not only in terms of holy individuals but also in terms of a holy church. Peter opens with: "Blessed be the God and Father of our Lord Jesus Christ! By his great mercy he has given us a new birth into a living hope through the resurrection of Jesus Christ from the dead" (1:3, NRSV). Peter also reminds them that, while they live the Christlike life in a world that doesn't always appreciate it, they are being "protected by the power of God" (v. 5, NRSV) even though for a temporary season they "have had to suffer various trials" (v. 6, NRSV).

It is interesting that many in the church these days seem shocked that we don't fit in so well anymore. For the people to whom Peter writes, it is their peculiarity that often becomes the occasion for their testimony when people watching their sanctified lives finally demand to know why they live as they do. In those moments they have opportunity to "give the reason for the hope" (3:15) that animates their lives. So what Peter says to these churches of Asia Minor in chapter 4, we may need to hear in our time: "Do not be surprised at the fiery ordeal that is taking place among you to test you, as though something strange were happening to you" (v. 12, NRSV). In fact, he tells them to rejoice that we share in the sufferings of Christ because in our faithfulness through times of trial is where the glory of God is revealed (v. 13).

The way our world has changed and is changing has thrown many Jesus followers into anxiety and stress. In these days of disequilibrium and change, the church too often reveals our lack of faith more than we reveal the glory of God. Whenever we place our hope in human leaders or governments to secure our lives or return us to former glory, we are revealing our weak faith. The danger here is that we become idolatrous. We begin to turn to the gods of business, government, or military power to lead us to the promised land when they cannot. The church of Jesus Christ is alive throughout the world not because the powers of money or military might have got it right. It is because, no matter what has happened, the people of God have embodied a different way. The body of Christ has willingly laid down its life in service not only to those who love us but especially to those who don't. We follow Jesus in this, who fairly defined our holiness as the graced ability to love our enemies and pray for the very ones who would persecute us (Matt. 5:44). The way forward for the church in our time is to listen to Peter's instruction. "Even if you do suffer for doing what is right, you are blessed. Do not fear what they fear, and do not be intimidated, but in your hearts sanctify Christ as Lord" (1 Pet. 3:14–15a, NRSV).

What does it mean to "sanctify Christ" in our hearts? This is essentially the same word used when Jesus taught us to pray, "Our Father in heaven, hallowed be your name" (Matt. 6:9, emphasis mine). It means there is nothing else and no one else in all the world that we trust for our life than the very One who made us and sustains us by grace. To sanctify Christ in our hearts is not something we can do by ourselves. It is Christ in us, expelling everything that is contrary to love. John Wesley said it like this: "It is love excluding sin; love filling the heart, taking up the whole capacity of the soul."[1] This is why Peter connects it to hope. Only when Christ is sanctified in our hearts do we have full capacity for hope, which is not wishful thinking for a better day; it is the present and firm conviction that the God "who raised [Jesus] from the dead and gave him glory" will also raise us so that our "faith and hope are set on God" (1 Pet. 1:21, NRSV).

I am challenged and inspired by a book from Alan Kreider called *The Patient Ferment of the Early Church*. Kreider, a church historian, is writing about "the improbable rise of Christianity in the Roman Empire." He notes that the early Christians were not attractional in the way we tend to think of it. They mostly tried to keep their gatherings secret and would let strangers in only after significant scrutiny. Because they were under such threat, they had to be careful. They did almost everything wrong to our way of thinking in terms of what it takes to grow the church, yet the church grew significantly in the first three hundred years. Their growth was not the product of a missions program, and they did not engage in conversations about mission strategies, yet the churches grew. They did lots of writing, but in the first three centuries they wrote nothing on evangelism or mission. What they wrote about was *patience*. They believed God was working powerfully in their worship and in their shared life to form them in such a way that the Christlike quality of their daily lives would become attractive and winsome to the people in their communities.

We get a snapshot of this in the well-known "Epistle to Diognetus," which comes from the second century and is a non-Christian's description of how these Christians were living. In part, it says,

They dwell in their own countries, but simply as sojourners. As citizens, they share in all things with others, and yet endure all

---

1. Wesley, "The Scripture Way of Salvation," *Works*, 6:46.

things as if foreigners. They marry [and] they beget children, but they do not destroy their offspring. They have a common table, but not a common bed. They are in the flesh, but they do not live after the flesh. They pass their days on earth, but they are citizens of heaven. When punished, they rejoice as if quickened into life. They are assailed by the Jews as foreigners, and are persecuted by the Greeks; yet those who hate them are unable to assign any reason for their hatred. To sum up all in one word—what the soul is in the body, Christians are in the world.[2]

Our forebears focused on forming their people in a *habitus*,[3] a way of being in the world that was so radically different from contemporary culture that it would compel people to ask why they lived as they did. That's when Peter's advice becomes so important: "Always be prepared to give an answer to everyone who asks you to give the reason for the hope that you have" (1 Pet. 3:15). In our time, we often seem to think of "give the reason" or "give an answer" as the work of rational discourse, perhaps even debate. The first Christians did not seem to understand it this way. One of the bishops of the early church said it like this: "Beloved . . . we are philosophers not in words but in deeds; we exhibit our wisdom not by our dress, but by truth; we know virtues by their practice rather than through boasting of them; we do not speak great things but we live them."[4] This is a picture of holiness of heart and life.

How is the contemporary church doing with this? In what ways are we embodying the life of holiness so that the Christlikeness of our lives becomes evangelistic? Are we living in ways that are interesting and attractive to those who are not following Jesus? Is the evidence of our lives that we are just as driven as everyone else to pursue the good

---

2. Mathetes, "The Epistle of Mathetes to Diognetus," *Early Christian Writings*, http://www.earlychristianwritings.com/text/diognetus-roberts.html.

3. Thinking here of the work of James K. A. Smith in the *Cultural Liturgies* series.

4. Cyprian, Bishop of Carthage (AD 256), quoted in Alan Kreider, *The Patient Ferment of the Early Church: The Improbable Rise of Christianity in the Roman Empire* (Grand Rapids: Baker Academic, 2016), 13.

life, even if it means mortgaging our peace on the altar of material-ism? Is our daily speech in the marketplace and neighborhood driven by the politics of fear, protection, and suspicion? Or is our conversa-tion "always full of grace, seasoned with salt, so that you may know how to answer everyone" (Col. 4:6)? Does our social media presence reflect the spirit of Jesus, or does it reflect the spirit of our age?

What would be attractive and compelling to people in our world is a group of people who live together and in the world in such a way that it begins to reflect the peaceable kingdom of our Lord Jesus Christ. The truth is that too many of our churches look more like the anxious and angry world than like the new creation. Perhaps what we need more than anything these days is revival that is not first about experiential fervor, but revival that is first about being deeply formed into the character of Christ Jesus. This is done in *prayer*, it is done in *worship*, it is done in *discipleship*, it is done in *education*, it is done in *fellow-ship*, and it is done in *serving*—but none of these things for their own sake. All of them, everything we are and everything we do as the people of God, must be surrendered to the lordship of Jesus Christ. We need our churches to be sanctified, set apart for the holy purposes of God. We need our churches to consecrate themselves fully by the grace of God, to surrender all our plans and ideas to Jesus, and to pray that God in mercy will come and fill us with the Spirit of Christ. We need Christ to "re-member" us, to unite us, so that we are saved from our individualistic, self-interested, prideful, and arrogant culture until we are redeemed, restored, and sanctified as God's holy people. As I have written previously, "The movement of true holiness people is never to isolate from the world in self-protective worry but to engage the world in confident hope. It is hope born of the conviction that there is enough power in the death and resurrection of our Lord Jesus truly to transform life—not only the lives of individuals and commu-nities but the very creation itself."[5]

---

5. Rowell, *Thinking, Listening, Being*, 89–90.

8 SERMONS

With a considerable sense of trepidation, I now offer several sermon manuscripts. I assure the reader that this is done with no sense of hubris that my sermons are particularly worthy of emulation. I am doing this because I believe that one way we become better preachers is by reading or hearing the preaching of others.

It may be that reviewing these sermons will inspire confidence that your preaching is just as good as, if not better than, the guy writing the book! If this is the case, I will be thankful. And if there is something here from which you can learn or even borrow for your own preaching, then I will thank the Lord.

Please note that these are written for preaching, for saying out loud. Therefore, the construction of phrases may be more casual than what would be the case for other writing.

This was a series of holiness messages preached during the season of Lent in the Christian year. The movements of the *paschal* journey, as experienced in the life of our congregation, seemed to be a fertile opportunity for hearing Scripture's call and promise toward holiness of heart and life. The title of the series was "Holiness: What Our Hearts Desire."

Sermon #1: The Big Lie
Genesis 2:15–17; 3:1–8

Okay, true confession time. How many of you would admit to ever watching Oprah? I don't think I've ever watched Oprah of my own volition, but I have walked in the house a few times when my daughter was watching. Frankly, most of what I've seen is not very interesting to me, but one thing caught my attention. It's the spirituality segment that apparently she has in every program. Do you know the title? "Remember your spirit."

"Remember your spirit." Sounds good. It may even sound Christian to those of us who are comfortable with the language of spirit. But in truth, what is this brand of spirituality that has become common in our culture? Jacqueline Hale, editor of a publication called *Living Life Your Way* (which is a clue), describes it like this: "We have obviously neglected our spirits for so long that now that they are crying out to be . . . heard. It's easy enough to recognize. It is goodness and all that is positive in your life. Relearn how to trust yourself and the many urges, little voices, and gut feelings you have every day. Go with your gut feelings. Act on your hunches. Consider the little voices. Don't question. It will change your life forever!"

There you have it: postmodern spirituality. What it really boils down to is that you are the master of your universe. You make yourself happy, and you make yourself healthy. Take care of yourself, have it your way, don't let anyone get in your way. It's all about you! So what's wrong with that?

Well, the Bible passage we've heard today wants to give us a major clue about what's wrong with that. And the clue has to do with how God really intended life to be for us and what happened to foul things up so badly. You and I now live in a world that certainly has some wonderful things and even happiness to offer, but at the same time is filled every day with broken hearts, hatred, murder, vengeance, deceit, abuse, death, and the vilest acts that continually press the boundaries of decent human imagination. And "remember your spirit" is supposed to fix that? You see, what contemporary, feel-better prophets don't understand is that the ache of our hearts will never be fixed through a process of personal, spiritual enlightenment—because that's not the problem. It's not a lack of knowledge. The problem is that something so basic to our life has been so broken that only God can fix it.

The problem is what I am calling today "the big lie." It's a lie that has confounded us since the beginning of our story. It's a lie that we continue to believe generation after generation, age after age. Our text for today paints the picture of how the big lie ever got a death grip on humanity in the first place.

You probably know that the book of Genesis is about beginnings—that's what the word "genesis" means. It's about the creation of the world and all that is good. The crowning achievement of God's creative work comes when God says, "Let us make mankind in our image, in our likeness" (1:26). And God created us, male and female, in God's own image. What does that mean, in *God's image*? To be created in the image of God means that we, unlike all the other creatures of earth, have the capacity for a unique quality of relationship with God.

So we come to chapter 2, verse 15, where we started our reading today, and we find God and the first man and the first woman living in that relationship together. We hear that God made provision for them. In fact, God gave them three things. One, God gave them work to do. God told them to work the garden and take care of it. Two, God gave them freedom, saying, "You are free to eat." And third, God gave them a boundary, saying, "There is one tree you must not eat from." (Note to the preacher: these ideas are drawn from Walter Brueggemann's commentary on Genesis.)

Did you catch it? God said, "You are free to eat from any tree." Now, that wasn't entirely true, was it? Because God turns right around and says, "Your freedom is limited by one thing. There is a tree in the middle that you must not eat from." In fact, God says to them, "On the very day you eat of it, you will die." That's a pretty serious boundary, don't you think?

Now, do you wonder what I wonder? Here's what I wonder: why would God place such a dangerous tree in the midst of his perfect garden? Why risk messing everything up? Why would God place this prohibition in front of his new companions when he knew good and well they were made from dust?

We have all kinds of good food in our kitchen. We have fruit, we have vegetables, we have nutritious, healthy stuff that our family can eat. But you know what we do when we go into the kitchen looking for a snack? We find the cookies! This seems like putting a plate of chocolate chip cookies in front of an eight-year-old boy and saying, "Now, listen, I'm putting these cookies here, but I don't want you to eat them. You can eat anything in this kitchen except those cookies." That doesn't seem fair, does it? I know good and well what that eight-year-old boy is going to do. In fact, I know good and well what I would do! I'm going for the cookies!

So why in the world would God give them everything and say, "You are free to eat it all" and then turn right around and limit their access to this one tree? Why? Because being created in the image of God is about relationship. And there is no true relationship without true freedom. And there is no true freedom without true choices. There is no cheap grace here. This is the kind of relationship God desires with us: true, honest, free, risky, and vulnerable. It's the atmosphere where true love can flourish.

But we move into chapter 3, and something begins to go terribly wrong. The crafty serpent is introduced, who begins to bring doubt into their minds. "Did God really say, 'You must not eat from *any* tree in the garden'?" Did you hear it? The serpent twists God's words just enough to miss the point. That's really not what God said, but doubt is raised. So the woman reports more accurately what God really said: "Eat from the trees, just not the one in the middle, or you will die." In fact, in the heat of the moment she adds a bit to what God really said. She tells the serpent that God said if they even *touched* the tree they would die. That's not really what God said, is it? Uncertainty, second-guessing, confusion—the door is open.

Isn't that kind of how it works with us? "Well, let's see, what did God *really* say? God wouldn't really mind if I did that, would he? Surely *this* isn't what God was really talking about. We have a fancy name for that: rationalization. Now here's where the big lie comes in. It comes from the voice of the serpent in chapter 3, verse 5. Here it is: "You will be like God."

Our first parents bought that lie, and we've believed it ever since. It has brought nothing but heartache and suffering because the truth is, we were not created to be our own god. We were created to live in perfect relationship with God, and every healthy and good relationship has boundaries. My marriage has boundaries. They are boundaries of love and trust that create a life of freedom and joy.

But suddenly, in the midst of this doubt, God's good boundary becomes a barrier to overcome. Eve begins to believe that God is holding her back. "The woman saw" that the tree was good and pleasing and desirable. Does that sound familiar? *Whatever makes you feel good, be true to yourself, listen to your own spirit.* Eat, even though God said no. It sounds like freedom, but the truth is, when we work so hard to free ourselves from all attachments, we are left with enslavement to ourselves. It seemed to our first parents like self-actualization. In reality, it was the tearing of a relationship of trust that, from this moment forward, could never be the same.

The way the Bible puts it is: "They realized they were naked." That means much more than that they noticed they weren't clothed. It means that in this moment, when they decided they could act as their own god, they became totally undone. Broken. Estranged. Sinful. Filled with shame. From that moment on, every one of our ancestors right down to us has been born into a broken and fallen world. Sin came, and nothing has been the same ever since. It impacts everything. We're in a mess. I don't know of any thinking person who would deny that. But the answer, the way out, the way to make it better, is not so weak as "remembering your spirit." We need a relationship to be restored. What we need is holiness. Yes, holiness. That's not some kind of extra add-on for super-saints. Holiness is the restoring of relationship between us and God the way God intended it at the start.

And this is where the gospel word comes. After Adam and Eve's sin, they know that everything has changed. They are ashamed, and they try to hide from God. They try desperately to cover themselves. It's a picture of what we have been doing ever since in the human race. We are desperately trying to cover ourselves, make our own way, find our own peace. But here's the good news. While Adam and Eve are hiding, God comes to them and calls out, "Where are you?" And ever since, God has been seeking us out, calling to us, "Where are you? Come home; come back to me."

In the midrash, which is the Jewish commentary on the law, this episode is referred to as "the first tear." Interesting connection. Adam and Eve mismanage the tree and, in doing so, unleash a torrent of tears across the millennia of human pain, suffering, and sin. But when we go to the end of the Bible—Revelation 22—the tree is there again. The tree of life is in the middle of the new Jerusalem. And Revelation says, God "will wipe every tear from their eyes."

What our world struggles to understand is that the ache of our hearts cannot be fixed by our own efforts to be more spiritual or true to ourselves. We need a Savior, someone who can restore us to a relationship of total trust, living safely within God's gracious provision for us.

We need someone like Jesus.

Sermon #2: We Desire a Holy God
Leviticus 19:1–2; 20:7–8

I was about the age of twelve when I really started trying to figure it out. I was raised in the church, particularly in the Church of the Nazarene. I'm fourth generation in this movement. I came up in the church with a certain vocabulary. We had a way of talking in the church, certain words that we used that were peculiar to church. Just as I learned a special vocabulary for baseball, I also learned one for church. In baseball, I learned terms like can o' corn, gapper, meat hand, and a buck-fifty-seven—that was my batting average! In church we said things like Redeemer, blood of the Lamb, salvation, total consecration, and holiness.

Holiness. That one always intrigued me. Growing up in the Church of the Nazarene, I knew quite early on that holiness was a very important word to us. The saints of the church said it with reverence and awe. Some, like Sister Garrett, wept when they talked about it. We sang about it at the top of our lungs: "Called unto holiness, church of our God . . ." For much of my childhood, there was a banner at the front of our sanctuary that had those words: "Called unto Holiness." I remember studying the denominational emblem that was always prominently displayed on our Sunday bulletin. "Holiness unto the Lord," it says.

I remember hearing the words of the scripture that we read together this morning. I heard these words quite often: "Be holy because I, the LORD your God, am holy." There's not really much to misunderstand there. It was pretty clear to me that God was calling me and that my church was calling me to be holy. But I knew me. I wasn't sure what holiness was, but I was pretty sure it didn't look like me. It looked more like old Charlie Griffith and Opal Mayhew and Mae Garrett and my grandpa—but not like me.

So here's what I figured out: holiness was something for older people who didn't have anything else to do but sit and pray and read the Bible. They were the ones that this word "holiness" was referring to. There was one problem with that. I also thought my pastor was holy, and he was only twenty-nine when he came to be our pastor; the Reverend John W. Wright. He had to be holy because when we had workday at the church on a Saturday he showed up in his wing-tips, white shirt, and tie and worked just as hard as the rest of us. I was in awe of him. I remember going into his study, age twelve, to ask if I could become a member of the church. He looked down at me, paused as if deliberating, and said, "Well, let's talk about that." I was scared to death! "Let's talk about that." That's all he said, but in those four words I became convinced that, somehow, he knew every bad thing I had ever done. I was about to flunk holiness at age twelve!

The point is that, having grown up in the church, I pretty much considered holiness to be a souped-up version of Christianity reserved only for those who had stopped struggling with the baser temptations of life. The really serious and highly religious folks could talk about holiness. And what I found out through my teen years, and then on into adulthood, is that I was not alone in that assumption. Holiness seemed so unattainable. So my generation changed the language; we modified the vocabulary. No longer did we want to talk about *consecration* and *sanctification* and *dying out to the old self* and *holiness*. We wanted to talk about *process* and *growing in your walk with Jesus* and *becoming more Christ-like*. These are not bad ways to talk; in fact, these are great ways to talk about what it means to be a Christian. But we have come to the place in our shared story where holiness is a word that many of us don't seem too comfortable with anymore. Some say it has too much baggage, too many negative connotations. And maybe it does. I have to admit that in my own experience it took a while before holiness could be a loved and cherished word rather than a dreaded and feared word. Fortunately, there may be something of a recovery underway, driven by the recognition that holiness of heart and life really is the beautiful invitation that God extends to us by the work of the Spirit.

Some years ago, we were singing, "Holiness, holiness is what I long for. Holiness is what I need." You know, it never would have dawned on me as a young person to think of holiness as something that I longed for. I only thought of it as something that was required of me, something at which most likely I would fail. Holiness was not my heart's desire; it was my dreadful obligation.

Now there is no doubt that God is quite serious about this business of our holiness. This word in Leviticus 19 is foundational to everything else the Bible has to say about holiness. The Lord says, "Be holy because I, the LORD your God, am holy." That is not a suggestion; it's a command, an imperative: "You be holy." And it comes in the midst of a rather overwhelming list of do's and don'ts. The context of this verse in 19:2 is a litany of wicked acts that will cut off the people from relationship with a holy God. Chapter 18 starts with, "You must not do what they do in Egypt or be like the people who now occupy the land of Canaan." Then the do-nots start, nearly thirty of them in chapter 18 alone. Then after 19:2 it starts all over again with the do-nots and the punishments associated with doing the do-nots until we get down to chapter 20, verse 8, and hear a hopeful word again. This may describe how many of us thought about holiness: a good idea surrounded by an overwhelming list of do-nots.

Loved ones, here's my essential plea to us today: let us not miss the point of God's call to holiness. It's really not about adherence to a list of don't do's. It is about recovering what was lost when sin entered the world. When we talk about being called unto holiness, it is not about behaving in certain ways. It is about the very character of God, who wants to answer our deepest heart's desire: the desire for life to be made right again, the desire to be at peace again, the desire to have hope again. Holiness is not first about our moral purity; it's first about the character of God. Holiness is about being restored to the image of God.

What I am trying to say to us during this series is that holiness is not an add-on; it's basic to what it means to be a Christian. Holiness is what can bring a sense of wholeness and well-being to your life because it's not about following a list of rules. It is all about being filled by the very presence of God in Christ by the power of the Spirit, so that everything I am and everything I do begins to be ordered by the Holy Spirit living in me.

There is no doubt that God's standard for us is high. "Be holy because I am holy" is about as high as it gets. And then Jesus sets the standard just as high when, in the Sermon on the Mount, he says, "Be perfect, therefore, as your heavenly Father is perfect." Now here's the good news: living up to that standard is not a matter of your effort. The heart of the good news that we celebrate here every Sunday is that what God requires, God provides. God did not say to us, "Be holy" and then leave us to figure out how to do that on our own. God said, "Be holy" and then gave us his Son, who died for our sins and was raised from the dead to destroy once and for all that which defeats us. Making us holy is at the very heart of God's desire because God wants the very best for us. Holiness is what our hearts desire because we desire a holy God. We desire a life and, ultimately, a world that is ordered and sustained by a God who—in the very essence of his being—is holy, pure, righteous, and faithful.

That ache of heart is something every person in this world feels. They might not define it as a hunger for God and his holiness, but that's what it is. We try hard to fill that void, that empty place, that ache of soul with all kinds of things. And we have so many choices these days, but nothing answers our need like having our holiness restored.

Would you consider these questions?

- Do you ever wish you could finally get on top of things spiritually, instead of feeling like a constant failure?
- Do you ever wish you could be confident and sure about where you stand with God?
- Do you ever wish you had the power to make the life choices you'd really like to make and live the life you've always dreamed of living?

If these are your desires, then holiness is for you! For the next few weeks I hope we can look very specifically at what it takes to enjoy the holiness God designed for us. For now, let us remember these simple things:

- God is holy and commands us to be holy.
- God provides what God demands (20:8).

- Holiness is a gift of God's grace that is given in a moment of faith.
- Holiness is a lifelong journey of spiritual maturity.

At the age of twelve I couldn't quite get it, but as I grew up here's what I learned: holiness is not some special brand of spirituality reserved for super-saints. Holiness is the regular pattern of God's people who open their lives fully to the love and grace of a God who wants nothing more than to bring us home and make us whole.

Are you ready to go home?

Sermon #3: Jesus Desires Holy Hearts
Hebrews 10:1–10

"What does God want from me?"

This may be one of the most important questions we could ever ask. When it comes right down to it, what does God really want from me? If you pay attention to popular culture at all, it becomes evident that people have all kinds of answers to this question. Some people seem to think that if you're just doing your best, that's all God really expects. I was fascinated by the reasoning of actress Sophia Loren in an interview she gave to USA Today in 1999. When asked about her religious convictions she said, "I don't practice, but I pray. I read the Bible. I should go to heaven; otherwise it's not nice. I haven't done anything wrong. My conscience is very clean. My soul is as white as those orchids over there, and I should go straight, straight to heaven."

Well, many of the people I speak with don't seem quite so confident. In fact, many seem to believe that no matter how hard they try, they can just never quite measure up. And in truth we really can't "measure up." I mean, we heard last week in the passage from Leviticus 19 what God's standard for us is all about. Remember? "Be holy because I, the LORD your God, am holy." And Jesus himself didn't ease the requirement; in fact, he almost makes it sound worse in Matthew 5: "Be perfect, therefore, as your heavenly Father is perfect." Who's ready to go and get in the front of that line?

During this season of Lent, we are thinking about the holiness of heart and life to which God calls us. But who can be holy? Isn't that a word that only belongs to God? And who can be, to use Jesus's word, perfect? One of the things we like to say the most to explain our foulups is, "Well, nobody's perfect." The apostle Paul says in Romans 3, "There is no one righteous, not even one." It would be a lot better if we could just compare ourselves to each other instead of to God. That way the spiritual standard becomes, "Can I live at least as well as most folks? Can I be better than average?" But what we've heard the last two weeks is that the standard we have to answer to is a lot tougher than,

"How do I compare to you?" The standard is the very character of a holy God. Who can stand up to that?

Thomas Aquinas, a great theologian many centuries ago, created one of the greatest intellectual achievements of western civilization. He wrote a massive work called *Summa Theologica*. His goal was to gather into one coherent whole all of truth. How's that for an undertaking? He was a brilliant man. He wrote in the disciplines of anthropology, science, ethics, political theory, and theology. But in 1273, Thomas suddenly stopped his writing. He was in worship one day when he caught an unusual glimpse of the otherness and holiness of God. Suddenly he knew that all his efforts to describe God fell so far short that he decided never to write again. His secretary tried to encourage him to do more writing, but he said, "I can do no more. Such things have been revealed to me that all I have written seems as so much straw." He didn't write another word and died a year later.

Who can stand up to the perfection and beauty and righteousness and truth and holiness of God? Not me. Not you. And yet God says, "Be holy, like I am holy." And so, across time, the story of God's relationship with God's people is often a rather sad tale of people struggling to measure up, working hard to figure out how in the world we can possibly be found acceptable in the sight of a God like that.

Well, the writer of Hebrews is speaking to a people who know that story very well. They are part of a tradition in which their ancestors received God's call to be holy and, along with that call, received the law that essentially said, "this is what holy looks like." The law set the standard. The Ten Commandments and all the requirements coming out of the commandments stood as constant condemnation to a people who were never able to discipline themselves into holiness. So we see God's grace in giving them the chance to come before him with sacrifices and offerings, that they might recognize God's holiness and their sinful condition, and receive forgiveness from God. And for centuries that's how it worked. Year after year, as the text says, the sacrifices of the old system were repeated. People made their pilgrimage to the temple to offer their sacrifice.

It really was a grace, but it was also a burden because, as the first four verses of today's passage say in the New Living Translation, these sacrifices "were never able to provide perfect cleansing for those who came to worship. If they could have provided perfect cleansing, the sacrifices would have stopped, for the worshipers would have been purified once for all time, and their feelings of guilt would have disappeared. But instead, those sacrifices actually reminded them of their sins year after year. For it is not possible for the blood of bulls and goats to take away sins."

Now here's the connection. We obviously don't sacrifice bulls and goats in an effort to please God and find relief from our guilt. But even now, we can so easily carry that same mindset with us into our relationship with God. And even though we know forgiveness is through faith in Jesus, some of us still believe we can never measure up. All of us, no matter how spiritually mature, probably experience those times once in a while. The real tragedy is that some Christians live there all of their lives. Maybe you live there.

We can become so convinced that we can never measure up that we live in a constant state of accusation and guilt before God. God says, "Be holy." Jesus says, "Be perfect," and we throw up our hands in defeat. There are a lot of people who think Christianity is nothing more than a constant reminder that you're not good enough. Too many people leave church every Sunday feeling condemned and undone, never moving to grace and forgiveness. Many have given up on church altogether because they think God is nothing more than a crotchety old man with a list of rules you can't keep, and then he'll just get mad at you when you can't keep them! Who needs that? This way of thinking is really not much different from what the writer of Hebrews is talking about. Just like our spiritual ancestors, we try to bring sacrifices with us. We line up our good deeds and hope to find them acceptable in God's sight.

"What does God want from me?" That's the question. And the answer that this preacher wants to give to the Hebrew Christians is, God does not want you to live under that endless drudgery. God is not interested in making us play some elaborate religious game where he sets a standard we can never achieve but kill ourselves trying to achieve.

Yes, God does command us to "be holy." And yes, God did create us to be holy, which simply means to be like him and live in relationship with him. But God knows what happened to us. He knows that sin entered the world. God understands that we are not able to get ourselves back to the way he created us to be. So God in grace did for us what we could not do for ourselves. And that's really what the book of Hebrews is all about. That's what this tenth chapter especially is about. When we were caught in a never-ending cycle of religious sacrifice, God provided the sacrifice to end all sacrifices. He gave us his Son. The good news here is that the never-ending cycle of sacrifices for guilt has been broken; it's over.

This was in the heart of God all along. God said through the prophet Jeremiah, "The time is coming when I will make a new covenant with them. I will put my law in their minds and write it on their hearts" (31:31, 33). God never intended for you to live your life in a futile attempt to be pleasing to him. God's desire for you was to bring you home. And that's why Jesus came and made the journey to Jerusalem. Jesus did not die to make you morally flawless; he died to make you holy. Big difference. Moral perfection is about adherence to the law. Holiness is about a heart of love.

Jesus does not desire from you moral conservatism. His desire is to give you a pure heart. Jesus does not desire from you attempts to think positively and overcome the hurts of the past. His desire is to give you true freedom from the past. He doesn't want your acts of service; he wants your heart to be so changed that you care passionately about people and serve them from a heart of love. He doesn't just want your disciplined devotional life. He wants to spend time with you as a friend who not only loves you—he really likes you! God delights in you. He loves being with you. This is the heart of Jesus. And this is the heart that Jesus desires. A holy heart. Hebrews 10:10, again in the New Living Translation, says it so simply and so well: "God's will was for us to be made holy by the sacrifice of the body of Jesus Christ, once for all time."

Loved ones, don't underestimate what God wants to do for you. Jesus did not die just to forgive and forgive and forgive a life of continuous failure and sin. Jesus died to make you holy. And if you will open your heart fully to him and release all your own effort to be pleasing to God, he will fill your heart with his Spirit, and he will make you holy. This is what God wants from you.

Sermon #4: Jesus Makes Holy Hearts
Hebrews 10:11–18

When I was six months old my family moved into an old, nineteenth-century clapboard house that gave new meaning to the phrase "fixer-upper." I don't remember, of course, most of the early work. I've heard the stories of how we lived in the midst of dust and the inconvenience of remodeling. My dad would work a full day at his regular job, come home, eat a quick dinner, and then work on that old house until late into the evening, catch a few hours of sleep, and start all over again.

By the time I was old enough to help, the jobs were better. By then we were building new things instead of tearing out old things. We built a back porch, decks, built out the basement, and put on a new roof. I was only about twelve when my father had me up on the roof of that two-story house, hanging on to full sheets of plywood until he could get up the ladder and help me put them into place. We worked hard. And it was fun. But there was always one point in the day to which I particularly looked forward. I never knew exactly when it would happen, sometimes in midafternoon if it was really hot. Sometimes it came later at night, but I knew the sign. At some point my dad would grab a cold Coke, go over by a tree or find an overturned bucket, and sit down. That was the sign. When Dad finally sat down, we knew the work was done for the day.

"He sat down." These words were spoken by the writer of Hebrews about Jesus in our text for today, verse 12: "He sat down." Those may be, in one sense, the most important words of the passage. We know from our focus last week that in this letter to Hebrew Christians, the writer is comparing the old covenant under the law of Moses with the new covenant under the sacrifice of Jesus. The writer contrasts the futility of the old sacrificial system with the perfect and completed work of Jesus. Before, the people had to bring animal sacrifices and offerings constantly because none of those sacrifices would ever take away their sins forever. But now when this priest, Jesus, offered for all time one sacrifice for sins, that was all we needed; the work was done. Nothing more could be offered, and nothing more needed to be offered. So, having made that perfect sacrifice, Jesus "sat down."

Did you catch the comparison? The writer opens this section by saying that the priests of the old covenant would stand, day after day, performing their religious duties. Standing is the posture of most priestly ministry. Even now we stand to lead worship; I stand to preach to you. We stand when the work is not yet done. We stand because there's more to do. For us, standing means readiness for action. We talk about lazy or unprepared people as "sitting down on the job." But Jesus "sat down."

It's interesting to notice how that posture even plays out in Jesus's ministry. I was interested to see just how often in the Gospels Jesus sat down on the job. In Matthew 5, at the opening of Sermon on Mount, the Gospel says, "He went up on a mountainside and sat down, and began to teach them." Later in Matthew's Gospel, the crowds have grown to unmanageable size. Once, the people gather on the lakeshore and press in so much that Jesus gets into a boat, sits down, and teaches from there. Why is this significant? It says something about authority. It says something about confidence.

I attended a pastors' conference years ago where our keynote speaker was Dr. E. V. Hill, the great pastor of the Mount Zion Missionary Baptist Church in South Central Los Angeles for nearly forty years. E. V. Hill was a formidable man both in physical presence and in personality. By the time he spoke to us, age was taking its toll, and Dr. Hill's balance was not sure. So when he came to address us they placed a wingback chair on the platform. I would feel constrained if I had to sit down to preach, but Pastor Hill came out, sat down, and held us with the power of his words for nearly two hours. Authority. Confidence. Jesus sat down.

In John 4 he sat down to engage in a life-changing conversation with the woman at the well. In John 8, just before the woman caught in adultery is brought to Jesus, the Gospel says he "sat down to teach them." In the book of Acts, the apostles follow Jesus's example. Going into the synagogues to try and bear witness to Jesus as the Messiah, they are often described as sitting down to teach. In this book of Hebrews it says on four different occasions, "[Jesus] sat down at the right hand of God."

"He sat down." It says something about a completed work in which there is so much confidence that nothing else needs to be done. All other work is over. In the past, every time the Israelites sinned, they had to present a sacrifice to atone for their sin. Even though we have not lived under the Jewish system of temple sacrifices, we can all relate to how frustrating it is trying so hard to please God by just doing good things. It can never be enough, and that is why Jesus came. God loved us so much, and desired relationship with us so much, that he was willing to win us back and bring us home. So "our High Priest offered himself to God as a single sacrifice for sins, good for all time. Then he sat down . . ." (Heb. 10:12, NLT). The work is done.

Now that's not all. He sits, but also "he waits." Did you see that? Verse 13: "Since that time he waits for his enemies to be made his footstool."

"The war has been won and now the mopping up is taking place. The victorious Son is waiting for all of his enemies, all of the manifestations of sin—disease, poverty, warfare, hunger, loneliness, anger, despair . . . even the final enemy, death—to be made a footstool for his feet."[1]

And "he waits"—which, again, is a picture of rest and confidence and authority. The end is sure, the outcome is certain, and we are part of that. God is not in a panic over the condition of our world. Christ is not anxious about what's going to happen to us. The work is done, the new creation has begun, and we are a part of that when by faith we trust our lives into the care and keeping of Jesus.

And as great as that is, it's still not the end of what this text says to us; there is more. Not only has Christ made the one sacrifice for all time, and not only is our future certain, but Jesus is also doing an

---

1. Thomas Long, *Hebrews, Interpretation: A Bible Commentary for Teaching and Preaching* (Louisville, KY: John Knox Press, 1997), 103.

amazing work in his people now. Here it is, verse 14: "By one sacrifice he has made perfect forever those who are being made holy."

Remember what we've heard the past couple of Sundays about what God wants and expects from us? God said, "Be holy because I, the LORD your God, am holy" (Lev. 19:2). Jesus said, "Be perfect, therefore, as your heavenly Father is perfect" (Matt. 5:48). Impossible commands, right? But listen to the gospel for today: "[Jesus has] perfected forever all those whom he is making holy." Jesus *has* done for us and *is* doing for us what we cannot do for ourselves. Praise be to God! "He has made perfect forever those who are being made holy." This verse is the climax of all that the writer of Hebrews is trying to say.

Now I know the question we have is, *How does this work?* Because I know I'm not perfect, and I don't think I've ever met anybody who was perfect. And it sounds contradictory. He has *made* perfect (which sounds like it's done) those who are *being* made holy (which sounds like it's ongoing). This is critical for understanding what holiness is. First, we need to understand what the Bible means when it says "perfect." It's not the same as when we use the word. In our Western and modern ways of thinking, "perfect" means "flawless." That's not what the Bible means. The Bible word is *telios*, which essentially means "to fulfill the purpose for which you were created." Can we be flawless in our walk with God? No. Can we fulfill the very purpose for which we were created? Yes, we can. What is that purpose? Jesus put it like this: "Love the Lord your God with all of your heart, mind, soul, and strength. And love your neighbor as yourself" (Matt. 22:37, 39).

Jesus "has made perfect." What does this mean? It means that through the sacrifice of Jesus, once for all, you and I can live the way God created us to live in the first place. With the tyranny of sin gone, with guilt gone, with our brokenness healed, we can love from pure hearts. That's what it means, according to the Bible, to be perfect. Then the text says, "those who are being made holy." Well, is holiness something that happens to me all at once, or do I kind of grow into it? The answer is yes. In a moment of faith, of trusting Jesus's sit-down work instead of my stand-up work, I am filled with his Spirit, and I am, by God's grace, sanctified, set apart, made holy.

But this is just the beginning. As Dr. Jerry Porter would say, "It's like the on-ramp to the highway of holiness." There is a journey of becoming more and more like Jesus so the world will see through me what it's like to be restored to the image of God. This is so important—please don't miss this. God calls us to be holy, we've seen that clearly. But you can't make yourself holy, which is why Jesus came. There is no longer any sacrifice for sin. It's not about your good works. It is not first about your devotion, your service, or your moral purity. You can't earn your way to favor with God. What you can do is trust the mercy and grace of Christ.

We seem to understand that becoming a Christian is a free gift, but then we seem to think that sanctification is about our discipline and work. No. It's still all about Jesus. Jesus does call me to a life of excellence, purity, sacrifice, and love. There is some discipline involved, but discipline is not what makes me holy. Jesus makes me holy and then gives me the power to live like he did. That's why the writer of Hebrews says it this way. He *has made* perfect forever (it's Jesus's complete work and gift) those who are *being made* holy (we are on the journey of Christlikeness.)

When my dad sat down at the end of a long day's work, I knew the work was done. Time to rest. Time to enjoy. Time to renew. Jesus sat down. The work is done. Now it's time to receive and enjoy and respond with a life of grateful service to the one who made this possible. This is different from becoming a Christian. When I become a Christian I ask God to do for me all I know needs to be done; I need my sins to be forgiven so I can be restored to relationship with God. But once I am restored, I begin to see that my need for God's grace goes deeper than having my sins forgiven. I need my heart to be changed so I can please God not because I try hard but because Jesus's sit-down work fills me and empowers me for life and for service.

Sermon #5: Jesus Keeps Holy Hearts
Hebrews 10:19–25

Across the weeks of this Lenten season, we've been focusing on the fact that God calls us to be holy. And not only does he call us to be holy, but he also provided for us, in Jesus, the way to become holy. To be followers of Jesus is to live a life of holiness. I don't know what comes to your mind when you think of holiness and your name in the same breath, but I think we think that holiness is such a high and lofty ideal that it must be unattainable in this life.

I hope you now understand that the Bible doesn't see it that way. I hope we have seen in these weeks that holiness is not an extra add-on for super-saints. It is the regular and normal experience of God's people who live under the lordship of Jesus Christ. In fact, as the title of this series tried to suggest, holiness is what our hearts really desire. Holiness is what we were made for because holiness means living as wholly (completely) God's, set apart for his purpose, sanctified. However, I wish we didn't so easily assume we are unable to live in the reality of holiness. We seem to think holiness may be a great idea but that, in the real world, you can't live there for more than maybe a few minutes at a time. There is a publication for pastors called *Leadership* that is famous for its cartoons. In one of my favorites, two couples are seated in a living room engaged in Bible study. One of the women is speaking and says, "Well, I haven't actually *died* to sin, but I did feel kind of faint once." I'm afraid that, too often, we think that's the best we can ever do in our battle against the influences of this world.

The message of Hebrews chapter 10—indeed, the message of the whole Bible—is that in Jesus Christ, God has made a way for us to fulfill his command, "Be holy, as I am holy." We have, the writer says, confidence to enter the most holy place. We've remembered during this Lenten journey that, back in the days of worshiping God in the Jewish temple, no one could enter the holy of holies. Only once a year could the high priest alone enter to make atonement for sins, and that was at peril of his own life. This was our situation before Jesus came. This was the despair of ever being able to please God and to fulfill his command to be holy. But then Jesus came and, in one of my favorite lines of Scripture that you've probably heard me quote many times in prayer here, is that Jesus has now opened up for us a "new and living way" (v. 20). Now we live inside the veil. That which was kept hidden is now open to us.

In our text for today, there is mentioned in verse 22 one of the most wonderful doctrines in the Christian faith. It is the idea of *assurance*. Because of Jesus, we can draw near to God "with the full assurance that faith brings." This is something that one of our spiritual forebears, John Wesley, struggled with earlier in his life. He spent years of his Christian journey struggling to know deep in his heart that he was accepted by God. One of the defining moments of his life came while crossing the Atlantic on a ship. A terrible storm came up, and he was terrified that he was going to die. But he also noticed a group of Moravian Christians on that ship who were remarkable by their peace in the midst of the storm. Later, he asked them about it, and what they wanted to know from Wesley was, did he have a deep and settled assurance that he belonged to God? That's where their peace came from. Wesley could not answer with conviction. He believed in God and that Jesus was the Savior of the world, but he really couldn't say much more.

Finally, one of the Moravian brothers asked him directly, "But do you know he has saved *you*?"

Wesley basically said, "Well, I hope so!"

The man asked, "But do you know yourself?"

And Wesley said, "I do." However, he would later write in his journal, "I fear they were vain words."

Some time later, Wesley went to a Bible study on Aldersgate Street. According to his own testimony, someone was reading Luther's preface to Romans. Wesley wrote in his journal, "About a quarter before nine, while he was describing the change which God works in the heart through faith in Christ, I felt my heart strangely warmed. I felt I did trust in Christ, Christ alone, for salvation; and an assurance was given me that he had taken away my sins, even mine, and saved me from the law of sin and death."[1]

Loved ones, there is no reason for our discipleship to be a life of uncertainty and fear. God wants to give us the gift of the witness of his Spirit. God wants us to be assured of our salvation, to know beyond doubt that we belong to him. The writer of Hebrews is talking about where that assurance comes from. It first comes from the Holy Spirit bearing witness, as promised in verse 15. But it also comes from knowing that Jesus not only *desires* holy hearts, and not only does he *make* holy hearts, Jesus also *keeps* holy hearts. A major part of holiness is not just living with a pure heart but also living with a confident heart. No fear. First John 4:18 says, "Perfect love drives out fear."

We have been given the good news that Christ is absolutely able to keep us safe and full of hope and bring us to heaven with holy hearts. What I want to know, Christian, is: Do you have this kind of assurance? Do you know deep in your soul that God welcomes you into the holy of holies? Holiness is about knowing that. We don't have a static doctrine of perseverance where, once I'm saved, I am always saved and don't have to think much about how I live. We have a dynamic doctrine of perseverance, where the Spirit of Christ indwells me, purifies my heart, and daily makes me able to stand in God's presence. Assurance leads to perseverance.

The writer of Hebrews says, "Let us hold unswervingly to the hope we profess" (10:23). Here is the discipline of the sanctified life. What does it mean to persevere? It means that, by God's grace, we make the choices each moment of each day that reflect a life lived in the unveiled presence of God. There's nothing to hide and nothing of which to be ashamed.

My father was an up-close model for me of this blessed assurance. Facing death far too early, my dad came to the end of his life with no worries and no fear. He came to the end from a life lived in honesty. His life was not flawless. I know some of the struggles of faith and re-

---

1. Wesley, *Works*, 1:103.

lationships that my dad experienced. But one thing was clear: because his life was fully surrendered to the Lord, he lived to the very last moment with confident assurance.

We are called to be holy, but don't ever get the idea that it's your work. Hebrews is clear that Jesus *makes* us holy and Jesus *keeps* us holy. So, verse 23, we live in hope. Not hope in the sense of, "I really hope that will happen," but hope in the sense of confident assurance. This is about trusting in the completed work of Christ who keeps us secure. Friends, I want to tell you today that there is no better place to live than that. And I think I can tell you from close observation that there is no better place to die than that. We are talking about the witness of the Spirit. Paul speaks of it in Romans 8 when he says, "The Spirit you received does not make you slaves, so that you live in fear again; rather, the Spirit you received brought about your adoption to sonship. And by him we cry, "Abba, Father. The Spirit himself testifies with our spirit that we are God's children" (vv. 15–16).

I grew up in a Christian family and in the church. My earliest memory is of trusting Jesus as the forgiver of my sins. But I soon discovered that I was headed for a life of Christian uncertainty, fear, and struggle unless God would do something more for me. As a young teen my parents explained to me in very simple terms the grace of entire sanctification. They explained that God could fill me with his Spirit, who would not only purify my heart but also empower me to live a Christian life. One night, kneeling beside their bed, I prayed a simple prayer of accepting that grace. I went to bed with a new sense of peace. The next day when I awoke, I still am unable to describe how everything was different. I was essentially the same person, of course, but there was a brand-new sense of belonging to God and of total assurance that the spirit of Jesus himself was living in me. I knew what Paul meant when he said in 1 Corinthians 2:12, "What we have received is not the spirit of the world, but the Spirit who is from God, so that we may understand what God has freely given us."

I'll ask you again: Do you have this blessed assurance? Do you know that Jesus has taken up residence in your heart and is giving you the power to live his life in this world? If you are a Christian, then to testify to anything less than that is to live beneath your privilege in Christ. Jesus wants you to be holy. Jesus is able to make you holy. And Jesus is able to keep you holy until he comes again.

Sermon #6: A Holy Life
1 Peter 1:13–16; Romans 12:1–2

I don't know if you've noticed, but when you are serious about being a follower of Jesus, this world just does not "get" you. What's more, the world is becoming less and less tolerant of you with your strange values and beliefs. Living a holy life in our kind of world is tough. But it's actually about much more than the way the world is. The issues are personal and specific. Some of the challenges you and I face this week will be challenges of personal integrity. How do I act in my workplace? Am I honest? How do I treat people? How do I spend my leisure time? What do I read, watch, listen to? Where do I go? How do I talk, what kind of conversations do I participate in? Do I pay my bills on time? How accurately did I fill out my tax return? Do I tell my parents I'm going one place, when I really intend to go somewhere else with my friends? When there's a choice between having things my way or doing things in a way that puts others first, what do I generally choose?

What does it mean to live as one who has been clearly called by God to be holy in the midst of a very unholy world? We may not often ask the question in just that way, but we deal with the question every day. We deal with that question every time we make decisions about what we are going to do today. We deal with it in every attitude and emotion we choose to express. We deal with it as we manage every relationship of our lives, from the most comfortable to the most distressing. This is everyday stuff. How do you live holy in a context that is so unholy?

The people to whom this letter is addressed have to face that question with sobering reality. This is written to a church under persecution. Peter writes to encourage and warn these Christians who are truly feeling like strangers in the land. Just like many Christians around the world today, they find the world a very dangerous place for people who believe and worship the way they do. I think we can relate to that. I don't know about you, but I regularly sense the danger of living as a Christian in a world like ours. So what is the word of instruction for them and for us? What does God's Word say about maintaining holiness in a pagan atmosphere?

Our attention almost immediately moves toward the specifics of attitude and behavior that the writer lists in this passage. And there is some wonderful instruction here. He talks about being disciplined and self-controlled. He speaks of finding our ultimate hope in Christ and in his grace rather than any kind of security this world has to offer. He talks about nonconformity to the sinful desires that once controlled our lives. He reminds us that our value must be in Christ and not in our annual salary or our important position or the acquisition of things. He goes on in the next part to speak of our love for each other as brothers and sisters in Christ and how that becomes a powerful witness to the world that we live by different values.

It's a wonderful list of characteristics that should be carefully considered. But I'd like to remind us today that in order for us to really live differently in this world, the work of God in our lives must go much deeper than the discipline of choices we make. Whenever we begin to talk about holiness it so easily gets reduced to the personal choices that I make, my private sense of morality and ethics, but it's a whole lot more than that. There must be a transformation of heart, a new birth of spirit that changes not just what we do but who we are as people. I think Peter understands this as he writes this heartfelt letter to his people.

You may have noticed that this passage begins with a "therefore," and you know what that means: we need to go back and see what it's there for. In the first part of the chapter, Peter has been reminding us of our life-changing relationship with God because of what Jesus Christ has done for us. He's talking about a radical transformation of our lives that is now possible because, verse 3, we have a "new birth into a living hope through the resurrection of Jesus Christ." We are not only saved from the brokenness of this world, we are saved to a life that, he says in verse 4, "can never perish, spoil, or fade" or be threatened in any way. Because when we unite ourselves to Christ by faith we are, he says in verse 5, "shielded by God's power until the coming of . . . salvation."

All of that is prior to the "therefore" of verse 13. I read it like this: in the first part of the chapter Peter says, "This is who you are," and then in our text he says, "Now act like it, and here's how!" Let me try and put the two together.

My assumption is that most of us here today really want to be authentically Christian. That's who we are; that's what we signed on for. But it's hard. The choices and dilemmas that seem so easily resolved on Sunday morning are sometimes so difficult out there where we live. I know that's true; I experience it too. But I want you to hear this morning what God's Word says. You can't be a holy Christian in an unholy world just by trying hard to act like one. It's more than simply being disciplined and careful. It's so much more than just being a good and moral person. The only way to live in the holy relationship that the Bible speaks of here is through a miraculous change of heart that is a work of God's grace. Stop asking, *What can I get away with and still be a Christian?* Stop asking, *How far can I go and still make it to heaven?* Start asking, *Lord, who do you want me to be? Look deep inside my heart and change what needs to be changed. Forgive me. Wash me. Fill me with your Spirit. Change my priorities. Change my attitudes. Empower me to do what is right.*

Where do you face the struggle of living a consistently Christian life? Many of you face it in your workplace. The pressures are great to compromise or at least to just be quiet. Some of you face it at home. Maybe you're the only one in your family really wanting to live like a Christian and it's hard when the people who know you best don't share that desire. Or maybe it's just the stress of contemporary American life that takes a toll on your family and you feel helpless to change it. A lot of you face it at school. I well remember the temptations and pressures I faced through school, and they're even greater for kids today. Many of you really want to be a Christian, but it's sometimes so easy to play the game of being one way at church or at home and another way at school. Some of you are struggling with being a true Christian not so much in the public arenas but in the private arena where nobody else really knows what you're up to.

Wherever you can relate to the real-life dilemma of being a holy person in a world like ours, here is the good news of the gospel this morning: God knows where you live. And God is *able* and *willing* to help you live a holy life. Both of those words are important. God is able—he has the power to help you do it. But he is also willing—God desires this for you. God isn't standing back with his arms crossed, saying, "Well, let's see how you pass this test." God is like a caring father teaching a child to ride a bike for the first time. He runs alongside you, with his hand gently on the seat to steady your wobbles, and he won't let go until you're ready to take off. And even then, if you crash and burn, he'll be right there to pick you up and dust you off and say, "Let's try it again." God's call to holiness is not a cranky, finger-pointing, "you probably can't do this anyway" charge. It's the best gift that a loving Father has to offer to his children. And everything you need to live a holy life has already been provided in the life, death, and resurrection of Jesus Christ.

Something I took away from my childhood was the oft-repeated reminder of my parents: "Remember who you are." That made a difference to me. And I think the Scriptures are really trying to say that to us as God's people: remember who you are. Be holy not out of your own effort but because it's the natural way for someone who is cherished by a heavenly Father who wants the very best for you. If all my parents had ever given to me was a list of expectations or characteristics I should have, it probably wouldn't have been all that effective when the pressure was on. Instead they gave me an identity, a vision for what a person of integrity was like. They gave me clear instruction by their words and mostly by their model of what it meant to live as one who belongs to Christ. So they said, "Remember who you are." I knew what they were talking about. And I wanted to honor those words because they didn't hand me a list; they gave me their heart.

And that is what God wants to do for us. The lists and expectations are helpful. We certainly do need God's instruction and commandments. But the only way we will ever really be able to live out those commands is out of hearts that have been changed and reformed by his love. Do you want to be a Christian who could honestly be called holy? Do you want to be a person of integrity and purity in the midst of sin and confusion? Don't concentrate only on trying to do holy things, but be made holy in Christ by giving the Lord complete rule and reign over every part of your life. Don't keep the Lord safely tucked away for Sundays. Allow him to enter every part of your life so he can cleanse you and form you and empower you to live a holy life.

Sermon #7: A Holy Church
John 17:13–23

Note: *Material from this sermon formed the basis for much of what is included in chapter 5 of this book.*

Much of my childhood was spent on the front pew of the Church of the Nazarene in a little lumber town in western Oregon. From my first-row vantage point, I witnessed my parents leading worship in various ways. My dad often led the singing, and my mom was our local missions president for most of my childhood. One of my vivid memories is of them singing a duet of a gospel song that was popular in those days called "On the Jericho Road." Part of the chorus says:

On the Jericho road

There's room for just two

No more and no less

Just Jesus and you.

I loved hearing my parents sing that song, but it never dawned on me as a young boy that it was really strange not only for that song to be presented as a duet but also that the whole idea of "room for just two" didn't fit with New Testament discipleship. And it's fair to say that at least part of the reason the error of that idea never dawned on me was that it never dawned on anybody who taught me the Christian way. My family and the congregation that nurtured my mind and heart in the life of Jesus until I was a young man taught me that the supreme concern was my personal relationship with Jesus Christ. I emerged from my childhood a committed Christian—but one who thought of discipleship mostly as "just Jesus and me."

Now, that's not all bad. I am deeply grateful that I learned what so many have not learned—that you can have a personal relationship with God through Jesus Christ. I have since learned, however, that community life is at the heart a Christian life. I understand that I do not walk this Christian journey alone. I am one member among many members of the body of Christ. In fact, I would now say that my supreme concern is not only for my personal relationship with Jesus

Christ but also that I might live as a true Christian within the community of faith so that together we might show the world what the kingdom of God looks like.

As we think about God's call to holiness, there is much more at stake than our personal holiness. A major part of this biblical call to holiness is that God calls his church to be holy. God is not only calling you to be holy; he is calling us, together, to be holy. However, many years of pastoral ministry have convinced me that, whenever we think about our walk with Jesus, we think mostly in terms of a personal and sometimes even a private journey.

There's room for just two.

No more and no less,

Just Jesus and you.

This individual mindset has some disturbing consequences. For example, there is in today's church a common lack of intimacy among God's people. We who speak of ourselves as brothers and sisters in Christ are, in fact, often not that close. Paradoxically, Christians are some of the loneliest people around. The cultural value of personal rights as supreme is often reflected in the church. Our society has driven home the idea that what matters most is individual rights. "Have it your way, protect yourself, actualize yourself, take care of yourself." This unchristian idea has thoroughly invaded the church. People leave churches every week on their way to different churches because, they say, "My needs just weren't being met"—as if this is the main reason to be part of a church. There is also a kind of "bootstraps theology" at work, whereby people seem to believe that being reconciled to God is mostly their work. "I" come to Christ, "I" get saved, "I" repent, "I" reorder my life, "I" surrender all. This rugged individualism in which we have become so steeped impacts every dimension of our Christian lives. It certainly impacts the way we think about and express the doctrine of holiness.

If we begin to think about how the church should be holy, it raises some different questions. Maybe holiness has as much to do with how *we* act and live together as it does with how I act and live individually. There is no doubt that the grace of God's sanctifying work is thoroughly personal. A life marked by the very character and spirit of Jesus is personal. But it is not private.

This is borne out throughout the Scriptures, but it is beautifully evident in the way Jesus prays for us just before he goes to the cross. This wonderful prayer in John 17 has the balance just right. Jesus does begin his prayer, interestingly enough, praying for himself. His relationship with the Father is personal. But it is not private, for Jesus quickly moves his prayer to the relationship that he and his Father desire with all who would believe.

Jesus's prayer for us is a corporate prayer, and as he prays for us together, one of the main things he prays for is that we would be holy. He prays in verse 17, "sanctify them by the truth." His longing is that somehow in our life together we might experience what it means to be a sanctified church. What does that mean? It means we are set apart, we are given a new and special identity and mission. It means we no longer live by the values and priorities of this world.

So he prays in verse 14, "They are not of the world any more than I am of the world." And yet, by his sanctifying grace, we are to live in this world as his distinctive people. Jesus prays in verse 15, "My prayer is not that you take them out of the world but that you protect them from the evil one." Jesus imagines more than a collection of holy individuals who happen to get together on Sundays. He imagines a holy church where the result is greater than the sum of the parts. Something powerful and new happens as God's people join together to impact this world as a people who, by the very quality of their lives together and their love for each other, make an eternal mark on the world and point people to a God of love and grace. So Jesus prays in verse 19, "I sanctify myself" (I set myself apart for a holy purpose— the cross), "that they" (we, us) "too may be truly sanctified" (set apart for a holy purpose).

Everywhere, the New Testament places the idea of a sanctified discipleship squarely within the context of the community of faith. Even as Jesus continues his prayer in verses 21 and 22 he says, "May they . . . be one as we are one." I think the important question then becomes, *How can a church like ours live that out? What does it mean, what does it look like for a church to be holy?* Let me suggest four ways that our church can be an answer to the prayer of Jesus.

The first has to do with worship. We've said before that worship is our central and core activity as a church. Everything else we are and everything we do must rise from our worship together. The reason I believe so many congregations fall short of living in holiness together is that worship becomes not much more than an exercise in personal preference. When worship becomes a matter of styles and forms and methods, we cannot live together in holiness. When worship centers more around individual concerns and preferences, there is no way it can honor God, who is always to be the object and the subject of our worship. (Marva Dawn asserts this idea in her book *A Royal Waste of Time*.) This is why it's important for our worship to be centered on the Word of God, organized around the story of redemption as re-membered in the Christian calendar, and energized by the Spirit who is present in word and sacrament to make us a holy church. Worship is essential.

The second way to be a holy church has to do with Christian forgiveness. Of course the larger issue is love, which is central to the whole idea of holiness. But I want to talk about forgiveness because what most damages authentic corporate holiness is unforgiveness. Forgiveness lies at the very heart of the gospel and at the heart of Christian holiness. If we really believe what we say we believe about holiness, then our relationships as brothers and sisters in Christ should not so regularly remain broken by unforgiveness. Holy churches are places where people are well aware that life together will inevitably lead to hurts and misunderstandings. But our pattern and our com-mitment when that happens is to extend grace, mercy, and forgiveness to one another. It's critical for a holy church.

The third way to corporate holiness is through a spirit of unity. Christian unity is the indisputable sign that the people of God have surrendered their own interests to the kingdom interest of serving

God and neighbor. It's a unity of the Spirit that says, "Even though we are so different from one another, and even though we have different ideas and different practices and different lifestyles, we belong to each other, and we need each other." This kind of unity crosses institutional, national, economic, racial, and gender barriers. Where holiness is active, the typical prejudices, discriminations, and suspicions between people are disempowered.

The fourth way to corporate holiness is through service. Corporate holiness is much more than a group of Christians being pious. It is the community of faith actively serving each other and engaging a broken world with acts of sacrificial love and service. It's living out the third statement of our mission that we remembered today, "God calls us to serve people as Jesus would serve, caring for the bodies and souls of our neighbors."

Certainly we could identify other ways that a church moves toward holiness in its life together. But these four are central and critical: worship, forgiveness, unity, and service. So how are we doing? Are we the kind of church where the spirit of Christ can move and work and cleanse and transform so that somehow in our corporate life we become an answer to Jesus's prayer? Are we remembering that our worship is not about our personal preferences but about the exaltation of Christ and the praise of God's glorious grace? Are we remembering that the gospel will never allow us to remain in broken relationships with each other? Is forgiveness active among us? Are we remembering that we can only be a holy church when we live in unity together, preferring one another above ourselves and laying aside petty differences for the greater mission? Are we remembering that our whole reason to exist has to do with those who are not yet a part of us? Do we remember that we are here not to serve ourselves but to serve lost and broken people?

I want to say, "Yes, we are a church that remembers these things." We certainly are not living there flawlessly. Sometimes we fail. But I do believe God is helping us be a holy church. Jesus prayed for us that we would be holy. He died and rose again to make us holy. He is working even now to make us holy. Let's be careful never to resist the work of Christ in our midst. Let's always be responsive and open, living in surrender to the lordship of Christ, not only individually but also together.

The truth is, on the Jericho road there is room for more than just two. There is room for all who join the company of redeemed and commit to walking together on this wonderful highway of holiness. Let's keep walking!

Sermon #8: A Holy Hope
2 Peter 3:8–13

Americans are big on insurance. We spend a lot of money every year on insurance policies of one kind or another to try to protect our possessions, our lives, and our loved ones. I suppose that's a good thing, but sometimes it goes over the top. For example, if you think you might be abducted by aliens someday, did you know you can take out an insurance policy against that? No joke. For $156 a year, a London company will insure you in the event you're nabbed by E.T. You've probably heard about celebrity insurance policies. Jimmy Durante insured his signature "schnozzola" for $50,000. Bruce Springsteen has a multimillion dollar policy on his voice. The chief taster for Edy's Grand ice cream insured his taste buds for $1 million. So what are you insured for? I know insurance has to do with managing risk, but doesn't it also at the core have something to do with fear? What are you fearful about? What are you fearful about losing?

Do you know there are some people who believe that Christianity is really nothing more than spiritual fire insurance? They believe the primary motivation for people to be Christians is that someday it might keep you out of hell. Apparently they can't imagine any other benefit, so it must be about spiritual fire insurance. I'll never forget leading a Bible study many years ago for young adults and hearing one young woman who had been raised in a wonderful Christian home say in absolute seriousness, "I'm a Christian for one reason and one reason only: I am terrified of going to hell."

I wonder, if we were all totally honest this morning, how many of us would have to say that at least part of our motivation for going the Christian way has to do with spiritual fire insurance? We read a passage like this, and it's pretty sobering. Peter seems to say that one day everything is going to burn, that the elements will melt in the heat and the heavens will disappear. Scorched earth. Our worst nuclear nightmare. So why wouldn't we want some insurance against that? Even this passage speaks of the "promise" that we who belong to Christ are looking forward to "a new heaven and a new earth." We call this Christian hope. We believe that in Christ we have a future and a hope, and that hope should and does impact the way we live in the present.

Now you might be asking, "Pastor, what in the world does all this have to do with holiness?" Glad you asked. The way you and I think about the future and respond to our present in light of that future has everything to do with holiness. You see, God's gift of holiness to us is not just one small piece of what it means to be a Christian. It's everything. It's not just about sins of the past being forgiven, or just about a flawed heart being cleansed; it is also about how we view the future. We are people of great hope. I think any Christian would say that, but the important question I want to raise for us today is, *What is it that we are really hoping for? How does God teach us to view the future?*

On this point not all Christians agree. Are we just hoping for a cataclysmic end to this sinful old world? Is Christian existence essentially a determined effort just to hang on 'til the end? Are we just counting down the hours until Jesus comes back and rescues us out of this world? A lot of Christians have pretty much believed just that. And, unfortunately, a lot of what you hear on Christian radio and read in the books you get from the Christian bookstore has that view. It goes something like, "This world is a broken mess; it's a sinking ship, and our job as Christians is just to survive and try to take as many people with us as we can before this old ship goes down."

But is that what the Scriptures teach us to believe about the future? Is that what it means to have Christian hope? If you really begin to understand what holiness is, then the answer must be no. When you believe that God is at work in the world, truly transforming people and the world through those people, then you can't see the future with anything less than radical optimism. We believe that God's grace is active in the world. His grace is active in the heart of every person, calling them to be reconciled and made new. His grace is active in believers, shaping them daily into the very image of Christ. His grace is at work in the church, helping us truly bear witness to the presence of Jesus in this world, serving as Jesus would serve, caring for the bodies and souls of our neighbors. Holiness says, *God is at work making everything new, making everything whole again.* So for Christians to have the idea that this world is just messed up and we can't do much more than wait for it to be burned up is to miss the power of what God is up to!

The Scriptures have quite a lot to say about the destiny of this world. Some of it is optimistic, and some of it is pessimistic. As people who believe a holy God is actively redeeming the world, we have an optimistic view. But I intentionally chose a text today that seems to least support that claim. It sounds like Peter believes what a lot of Christians today believe: "Hold on, the ship is going down, but Christ will rescue you just in time." There are two things I want you to notice. One, this is not all that Peter says. He does appear to say that creation is doomed, but then he talks about what our response to that fact should be. And the response he holds forth has nothing to do with just biding our time until Jesus comes back and destroys the evildoers. Our response is to be actively and energetically involved in what God is doing in the world. Look again at verses 11 and 12: "Since everything will be destroyed in this way, what kind of people ought you to be? You ought to live holy and godly lives as you look forward to the day of God and speed its coming."

"Speed its coming?" What does that mean? It has to do with the central point that Peter is actually making in this passage, which is, "Don't worry that Christ hasn't returned yet. He knows what a terrible mess the world is in, but the reason he hasn't returned is that he is patient and doesn't want anyone to perish." In other words, God is still on a mission to save the world. And if it's God's mission, then it's our mission. Holiness people do not have the luxury of giving up on the world. We roll up our sleeves and get to work sharing the good news of Jesus with everybody we possibly can, not just because we think the ship is going down but because we optimistically believe that God's grace is working to change lives and heal hurts and restore brokenness and make things new. So the first thing to notice is that Peter is not really pessimistic. He's realistic, but he is also positively optimistic about God's prevenient grace and our part in being conduits of that grace to a hurting world.

The second thing to notice is that many other scriptures speak differently about the future and our part in it. In Romans 8 Paul talks about the creation being liberated from its bondage. Colossians 1 talks about all things, whether on earth or in heaven, being reconciled to God through Christ. In Matthew's Gospel, Jesus speaks about "the renewal of all things" (19:28). And in Revelation the risen Christ says, "I am making everything new" (21:5).

The Bible is full of optimism about the ability of the gospel of grace to change the world. And if holiness people believe anything, that's what we believe. People really can change. Families really can change. Systems really can change. Nations really can change.

Loved ones, let me say it as simply as I can. God has saved us. And in Christ, God has made a way for us to be holy like he is holy. But that holiness does not make us fragile display pieces. It makes us fearless servants who run toward the "least of these" (Matt. 25:40). Our theology of hope compels us into the world to serve. We have real hope to offer those who have been abused by sin. We have real hope to offer our families, our neighbors, our communities, our nation, our world. God is in Christ reconciling the world to himself (2 Cor. 5:19)! Friends, do not accept a Christianity that is anything less than optimistic about the world. Do not accept a Christianity that has a sinking-ship mentality. God offers us a Christianity that has a transforming-power mentality, a Christianity that understands that our participation with Christ is literally changing the world.

The very best that insurance can ever do is provide a substitute for what was lost. Don't settle for the substitute. Live the real thing. As a person who has been redeemed by the power of God in Christ, go out and optimistically tell everyone you can that there is hope. Go out and believe that you really are changing your world by living as a faithful disciple of Jesus Christ.

■ A PRAYER FOR HOLINESS*

Father, thank you for your call. And we're sorry that we have so often heard it as a list of expectations being placed on us. We heard it as a burden.

Would you remind us today that your call to be holy is a call to come home and to have the deepest ache and longing of our heart filled?

Lord Jesus, please make us hungry to be holy. By the work of your Spirit in us, make us thirsty to be like you. And give us the grace, we pray humbly, to so surrender control of our life into your hands that you can begin to restore us to what you had in mind; people who reflect your very image.

Help us to respond by opening our hearts wide to you and by allowing you to do the full and complete work of your Spirit in us. This we pray in the name of Jesus Christ, our risen and reigning Lord. Amen.

*From the book by Tom Nees, Dirty Hands—Pure Hearts: Sermons and Conversations with Holiness Preachers (Kansas City: Beacon Hill Press of Kansas City, 2006), 130.